S0-BVN-963

Going Freelance

A Guide for Professionals

Robert Laurance

John Wiley & Sons, Inc.

New York • Chichester • Brisbane • Toronto • Singapore

This book is dedicated to
all of those professionals
who want to go freelance,
but who hesitate to take the step.

Take heart.

You can succeed!

The best is yet to come!

Publisher: Stephen Kippur
Editor: David Sobel
Managing Editor: Ruth Greif
Editing, Design, and Production: Publications Development Company

This publication is designed to provide accurate and authoritative information
in regard to the subject matter covered. It is sold with the understanding
that the publisher is not engaged in rendering legal, accounting, or other
professional service. If legal advice or other expert assistance is required,
the services of a competent professional person should be sought. FROM A
DECLARATION OF PRINCIPLES JOINTLY ADOPTED BY A COMMITTEE OF
THE AMERICAN BAR ASSOCIATION AND A COMMITTEE OF PUBLISHERS.

Copyright © 1988 by Robert Laurance

All rights reserved. Published simultaneously in Canada.

Reproduction or translation of any part of this work beyond that permitted
by section 107 or 108 of the 1976 United States Copyright Act without the
permission of the copyright owner is unlawful. Requests for permission
or further information should be addressed to the Permission Department,
John Wiley & Sons, Inc.

Library of Congress Cataloging–in–Publication Data

Laurance, Robert, 1950–
    Going freelance : a guide for professionals / Robert Laurance.
        p.   cm.
    Bibliography: p.
    Includes index.
    ISBN 0-471-63256-2.   ISBN 0-471-63255-4 (pbk.)
    1. Authorship. I. Title.
PN145.L28   1988
808'.02—dc19   87-28571
                                                                CIP

Printed in the United States of America

    10 9 8 7 6 5 4 3 2

ACKNOWLEDGMENTS

I would like to thank Bryce Webster of Leahan Webster Advertising & Marketing, who has worked as a successful freelance professional for more than 15 years, for her thoughtful comments and assistance. Thanks also should go to my editor, David Sobel, for his patience and excellent suggestions about how to improve the book and make it as meaningful as possible to potential freelance professionals.

CONTENTS

v

INTRODUCTION

You work as a professional. Perhaps you are an attorney, an architect, or an accountant, working in a large firm. You have succeeded, but you feel frustrated. You never get a chance to express your best ideas. You have not received salary increases or bonuses commensurate with the amount you *want* to earn. You are impatient; you do not want to wait another five or ten years until you become a "junior" partner in your mid- or late 40s. Most of all, you want to run your own show. You believe you have got what it takes to work independently and accomplish far more and earn far more money than you do working for someone else.

Perhaps you cannot quit your job today or tomorrow. Constraints of family, money, experience, training, and—let's face it— fear hold you back right now. You aspire to work for yourself, but you know it will take some time, some money, and a lot of planning before you strike out on your own. But that does not mean you cannot start moving toward your goal of independence now. You can.

You want to become a *freelance* professional, perhaps starting

1

part-time, but working toward becoming an independent professional. Although the term "freelance" was first used to characterize writers, artists, and photographers, it now applies to every professional who works independently. This book identifies 15 categories and more than 100 different professions or professional occupations in which you can work freelance, either part- or full-time. We do not claim to have identified even half of the possible freelance professions. Practically anyone working in a white-collar occupation or profession can use that experience to work as an independent freelancer.

≪ THE GOAL OF THIS BOOK ≫

This book aims to show employed professionals how to become successful freelancers in their own or directly related fields. It is *not* concerned with employees dissatisfied with their current jobs or careers and who want to change their jobs or careers. It is written for the professionals who have begun to think that they can achieve more on their own. The book defines freelancing and distinguishes it from other types of self-employed or independent businesspeople. The logical sequence is this: A freelance professional is both self-employed and an independent businessperson, but all self-employed and independent businesspeople are *not* freelancers.

Many professionals already work freelance without calling themselves that. They usually call themselves *consultants* or advisors. Even visiting nurses, who take temporary assignments, would be defined as freelancers. Independent accountants who work on their own or in a small, loosely organized professional corporation work as freelancers. Financial planners, mortgage brokers, bookkeepers, credit/collection investigators, graphic and commercial artists, independent computer programmers and systems analysts, court reporters, insurance investigators, consulting engineers, aerobics instructors, child development counselors, and dozens more all work as freelance professionals.

≪ FREELANCE VERSUS PART-TIME BUSINESS ≫

By definition, freelancers sell their skills and talents. They sell *brainpower,* not muscle or products. Freelancers differ from other self-employed or part-time businesspeople in a number of signifi·cant ways:

▶ They sell *professional* services dependent on their own experience, skills, talents, and background. They are almost always considered white-collar freelancers and, usually, the work requires a college education or advanced technical training. A person who starts a cleaning service or buys a home cleaning franchise and hires a team of minimum-wage workers to do the jobs would *not* be considered a freelancer. A team of television news photographers which drives the streets of a large city filming news events and sells that film to local television stations would be considered a freelancer team.

▶ They do *not* sell products made by other companies. A person selling cosmetics or kitchenware through party plans or door-to-door selling would *not* be considered a freelancer. A person who sells his or her services as a sales trainer to corporations would be considered a freelancer.

▶ They do *not* manufacture "hard" products. A homeworker who knits woollen goods for sale through a handmade crafts shop is not a freelancer; a marketing consultant who advises the crafts firm or crafts store how to market the knitted goods would be a freelancer.

▶ They do *not* have retail outlets or provide wholesale distribution. They may work out of an office or their home, but they do not open retail outlets or wholesale warehouses for the sale of goods. They do not change fields and buy franchises, even franchises related to their own fields. An advertising copywriter could buy a franchise that sells direct mail advertising to local businesses or prints a weekly giveaway shopper. That would not be freelancing. The copywriter would have to sell his or her services to an existing agency on an occasional or project-by-project basis to be considered a freelancer.

▸ They do work as active professionals in their own or closely related fields. An accountant, who had a hobby catching and smoke-curing eels and selling them to friends would not be a professional freelancer, but a hobbyist.

▸ They do not have large staffs or many employees. They may have an assistant or secretary, but they largely tend to work alone. An accounting firm with three partners and six assistants and bookkeepers would be a professional firm. An accountant who worked out of his home, prepared income tax returns for families, small businesses, and other professionals, and audited the books for local businesses would be a freelancer.

Difference between Freelancers and Consultants

In many respects, there are few differences between the services offered by freelancers and those offered by consulting firms. It is almost entirely a matter of size and degree. Pension and employee benefit consulting firms often have hundreds of employees and a network of offices. They would be considered consultants, not freelancers; a pension consultant who occasionally provided services to the firm in exchange for a retainer or flat fee would be a freelance consultant. The same holds true for management consultants, insurance risk prevention consultants, computer consultants, engineering consulting firms, and so forth.

≪ LEGAL ASPECTS OF THE FREELANCER STATUS ≫

The Internal Revenue Service (IRS) helps clarify our definition of freelancer in the ways it defines œelf-employment" and "independent contractors." The IRS considers all self-employed people to be independent contractors. Since all freelancers are self-employed, by definition, the IRS rules apply. However, the IRS has strict rules that determine whether or not you can be considered self-employed. Among the most important of these are:

▶ *W-2 and W-4 forms.* If you fill out a W-2 or W-4 form for a company, you are automatically considered an employee. A firm to which you provide freelance services should always file 1099-B forms reporting the total amount in fees you receive each year.

▶ *Benefit plans.* If you accept, sign up for, or pay for any benefit coverages, you are considered an employee.

▶ *Specific work hours.* If a company has the right to determine when, how long, and where you work, you are considered an employee. As a freelancer, you have to be able to do the work when, where, and how you want to, preferably away from a company's premises. You can temporarily use or borrow company facilities and offices, but you cannot be required to work from 9 to 5.

▶ *No assigned office.* You should not have an office set aside solely for your use. On occasion you can use an empty office or an office set aside for consultants, conference rooms, and the like. A sales trainer can use conference rooms or classrooms to present courses, but should not have a permanent office. You should develop your course materials in your own office or at home. You must set aside part of your home for *exclusive* use as an office, or rent space in professional or commercial offices, to be considered self-employed.

▶ *Own materials.* A firm can reimburse freelancers for supplies, materials, and expenses, but it should not provide, for free, those supplies and materials to the freelancer except when they directly impact his or her work. A freelance market research consultant may borrow company stationery to send out questionnaires for a survey, but the firm should not pay for the freelancer's private stationery. A systems analyst may borrow a computer terminal, but it would be far better for the analyst to pay for her own terminal and put it in her home or office.

In short, if you receive a salary or hourly wage and if your firm or company withholds federal income taxes, FICA (Social Security), or unemployment, disability, state and/or city income taxes from the money you earn, you will be considered an employee. If you have specific working hours, if you have an office or the company provides your place of work, if the company provides the materials, supplies, facilities, etc., where you work, or any combination of these, you will be considered an employee. In this book, we consider some interesting and controversial exceptions to these rules in detail, but these are the rules most often used to define self-employment or independent contractors. In addition, these are the rules used by the IRS and *that* is important!

The Essential Consideration: Money

Why do you need to follow these rules and procedures? The answer is simply one word—money. If you are considered an employee, you lose the ability to deduct the entire gamut of expenses considered normal and proper to operating a business. In this book, more than 40 categories of deductible business expenses which freelancers are eligible to claim are defined and discussed in Chapter 6. These perfectly legitimate expenses are worth thousands of dollars to you in income tax deductions—and consequently increased profits— each year.

Of course, although you can deduct these expenses, as a freelancer, you lose all of the cushy corporate "perks" and "bennies" (perquisites and fringe benefits) to which many professionals have become accustomed. Coping with the loss of the essential benefits, such as medical and hospital insurance, raises an important question when you think through whether or not you should become a freelancer. This is discussed in detail in Chapter 2.

≪ HOW TO MAKE THE MOST OF THIS BOOK ≫

This book will lead you step-by-step along the sometimes difficult path of becoming a freelancer. The first two chapters examine why you should freelance and how most people become freelancers and whether or not you, in particular, should become a freelancer. The second chapter considers the serious lifestyle issues that many potential freelancers overlook. Although it may seem specious, the question of whether you or your family can tolerate your presence in the house all day long should not be taken lightly. How to face working alone, if you have worked among large groups of people for years, is a similarly serious question.

Chapter 3 considers the question of qualifications and training. It gives not-so-obvious examples of how much and what kind of qualifications and training successful freelancers need in various professions.

Chapters 4 through 7 analyze the financial aspects of starting your freelance business—both part- and full-time—and building a successful "practice." That is a good term to borrow from the medical profession: Practitioner. Because it signifies what you have to do to succeed as a freelancer—practice your profession consistently and, if not expertly, at least competently. Although Chapter 6 discusses the myriad tax consequences of freelancing, Chapter 7 is the most important chapter of the book. Whether you know it now or not, you are about to become a salesperson. Most freelancers—at least the ones that consistently prosper—soon realize that they must sell their services again and again to existing and potential clients. In freelancing, there is only one rule: You are only as good as your *next* performance. Selling your services, promoting good customer relations, handling difficult customers, and *getting paid* by reluctant or even penny-pinching clients will take up more of your time than you can, at first, imagine.

Will the rewards be worth it? For tens of thousands of young and middle-aged professionals who have felt trapped in positions through which they could not achieve their personal goals, becoming a freelancer has enabled them to reach and exceed their personal and professional goals, often in ways they could never before have imagined.

I know. I have been a successful freelance journalist, author, and market researcher since 1977. I have written, coauthored, or edited 15 business and technical books, authored 20 book-length market research reports, consulted with many Fortune 500 corporations, and a foreign government, and written literally hundreds of articles for every kind of publication from *Boys' Life* to Auerbach Management Information Services. My salary (current gross income), even adjusted for inflation, equals significant multiples of my salary at the last job I held. I have done things and gone places that would have been out of the question if I had continued to work as a newspaper reporter. I have visited Europe eight times and become personally acquainted with fascinating people of every stripe and hue—from megamillionaire entrepreneurs to European nobility to a state trooper who catches and sells eels for part-time income. My decision to work freelance has created opportunities— business, personal, and social—that have far exceeded any that I could have expected from my previous career.

That is perhaps the most important and meaningful advantage of working freelance. Freelancing makes you available for and opens up opportunity in whatever form you want to create it. You do not have to go to Europe; perhaps your idea of opportunity is to sit on the beach four days a week. If you can use your time "catching rays" to think of ways to reach your financial goals during your three working days, why not? For example, an advertising freelancer in New York City decided one day to stop working and sail around the world. He had accumulated enough money from his work and wise investments to do this. Although he didn't make it around the world—his boat was wrecked in a storm off Ecuador— he did spend two years doing exactly what he wanted to do. But he wasn't financially or professionally ruined. Armed only with his experience and excellent reputation, he returned to New York and was soon back to doing work for the best clients in town.

His experience makes a very valuable point: Not only could he arrange his circumstances to fit his goals, he did not lose anything by doing so. He based his success on his brainpower, talents, and skills. He could take them with him anywhere he wanted to go. He had them when he returned to the active world of business. This is an incalculable advantage that freelancers gain and keep as long as they keep their skills honed and their brains primed.

Perhaps you do not want to sail around the world or become the world's leading independent authority on sales training. Perhaps your goal is simply to work freelance part-time to earn enough extra money to build a retirement nest income, pay for your children's college education, or set aside money so you and your spouse can have children without both of you continuing to work. This book carefully outlines this path, too. For example, one corporate attorney in New York carefully planned her future career as a full-time mother and part-time corporate lawyer like this: She had worked in the legal department for a major bank, but she wanted to freelance while she thought about starting a family. She first arranged to work in her office two days a week and take freelance legal assignments for the rest of the week. Gradually, over several years, she weaned herself and the bank away from her physical presence and into a full-time freelance effort. Today, several years later, she is busy weaning her first child, while continuing to work freelance for the bank. She could do this without disrupting her and her husband's lifestyle because he, also a corporate attorney, continued to work full-time for his own firm, as he wanted to do.

Last, but not least, this book provides in Part II an extensive resource guide for professional freelancers. It lists hundreds of associations and organizations to whom a professional can turn for help, provides dozens of listings of books, publications, and articles, and discusses sources of assistance for the 15 categories and dozens of freelance occupations.

In short, this book serves as your one-stop guide to starting and succeeding in your own professional freelance business.

« PART I »

WHAT FREELANCING IS ALL ABOUT

≪ 1 ≫

WHY FREELANCE?

There are as many reasons to freelance as their are freelancers. People make the decision to go freelance for their own unique combination of reasons. These reasons come from both their business decisions and personal desires as well as reasons that their families, employers friends, or changing circumstances, spawn. This book cannot give you a formula that you can apply because the decision to go freelance involves many "intangibles," the influence of which only you can weigh for yourself. We will note both positive and negative considerations. We will describe the most common reasons people decide to freelance. Then, in Chapter 2, we will discuss the personal, psychological, emotional, professional, business, and family influences and issues so you can then decide whether you are prepared to become a *successful* freelance professional. Note that the word "successful" is stressed. Anyone can quit a job and hang out a shingle that says "Freelance Whatever," but it takes much more to truly succeed over the long haul. Many people try freelancing and when clients do not rush to their doors, they quietly fold their tents and find new jobs. That is not the purpose of this book.

With the lessons in this book, you will have a framework with which you can become a successful freelance professional for the rest of your working life—and beyond into retirement.

≪ THE MAIN MOTIVATOR ≫

The primary reason most people freelance, at least part-time, is money, rather the lack of it or the desire for more. Engineers who donate articles to or take $50 honoraria for articles in professional journals are not true freelance professionals; they are hobbyists doing something they want to do or to obtain a feather to put in his or her career cap. An engineer who sells his services for $100 to $250 an hour and works at night and on weekends so he or she can pay for a college education, take a European vacation, or build a retirement nest egg, of course, is a serious freelance professional.

To paraphrase Samuel Johnson: None but a fool ever freelanced but for money. Freelancers are worthy of their hire and they know it, and they expect to be paid a reasonable rate in the open market for their services, skills, and knowledge. What they get paid, however, depends strictly on the markets they serve, or even segments within that market. My market research work pays at far higher hourly rates than writing individual articles. The former skill is in greater demand and shorter supply than the skill of writing magazine articles. Simply put, the freelance market works almost like pure capitalism, and your fees and charges depend directly on what the market will bear.

Publish or Perish

The second most compelling reason to freelance is that you must do so to enhance your professional standing and reputation. Perhaps your job has a limited set of duties which would never allow you to make a dramatic change in your professional level. You could—and may have to—take courses to expand your technical knowledge of your field. But the knowledge gained in your studies may not qualify you for the professional status you seek. You will have to gain work experience. This is the case for many accountants who want their CPAs. In addition to a test, many states require at least two or more years of work experience to qualify as a CPA. If your company has no plans to give you that experience, then you could freelance, doing the books, tax returns, and accounting work for small businesses and gain the required experience. (Note that some states require "slave labor" in an actual firm of CPAs before you qualify, but others count freelance work experience.)

Change Careers

A third popular reason to freelance is a strong desire to change careers. Perhaps you want to stop working as an accountant and become a commercial or graphics artist. If you could draw, or had taken the basic courses, you could freelance work at night and on weekends for local advertising and graphics agencies. You can accumulate experience so you can ultimately support yourself as a freelance graphics artist, find a top job as a graphics designer, become an artistic or creative director at an advertising agency, or start your own commercial art firm.

A corollary of career changing is preparing for activity after you retire from your current job. Many people serve in the Armed Forces, work in civil government, or simply go to work at an early age and stay with the same company for 20 or 30 years. They retire at relatively early ages, from 38 to 65, yet they want to continue to work, although they have pensions. Or perhaps their pensions do not provide a livable income because they are so young, and they must find a second career. You can more easily make the transition if you prepared for a second career by freelancing part-time during your first one. Some professionals, such as attorneys in the Armed Forces, are prevented from practicing their profession freelance, but they could practice a different one on their own time. In other cases, attorneys become CPAs and have a freelance accounting practice that does not interfere with active work in a law firm.

Strong Desire

Other people decide to freelance simply because they have a very strong desire to do what they want to do. They differ from hobbyists in that they believe in themselves and know the value of their skills well enough to demand adequate payment for them. Many people simply like to write books, give speeches and lectures, give advice as consultants, and provide their unique services to others. Perhaps they feel (and are) stymied in their jobs; perhaps their jobs don't present any opportunities for these means of self-expression; any motivation will do.

≪ REAPING THE REWARDS ≫

Just Plainly More Money

Frankly, most part-time freelancers start that way because they want more money. They want to buy a house, a car, a vacation cottage or a condominium, save for a child's college education, or pay off some bills. Either need or desire compels them to start freelancing. Most people who work outside sales do not have the chance to rapidly or dramatically boost their salaries or incomes from a job. Some managers and executives have stock options or receive bonuses, but usually these have legal or corporate constraints on how and when they can be exercised or received.

For most people, earning extra income relatively fast means taking a second job, working on weekends and at night. Usually, second jobs offer less money, challenge, purpose, and responsibility than a regular day job. A bookkeeper may work as a waitress; a corporate manager may own an ice cream shop. Generally, people with second jobs do not make maximum use of their professional skills and experience. This is not true of a professional freelancer. The bookkeeper would prepare tax returns and financial statements and the manager would offer seminars in his specialty to less experienced managers, or consulting services to noncompetitive companies. The difference is that, as professionals, they exercise and build upon their skills and experience to earn more income and gain greater rewards, such as an enhanced career and better reputation among their peers. But the extra income almost always comes first—at first.

Less Security Can Mean More Money

If Samuel Johnson is correct about money, as we believe he is, then a freelance professional can achieve more financial security by his independent work than by so-called "steady" employment. It does not appear this way. Many people have a dread of leaving a secure paycheck that is given to them every week or two. But this paycheck gives only the illusion of security. Consider the tens of thousands of layoffs that have occurred during the mid- and late-1980s as industrial giants downsized to meet competitive pressures. AT&T reduced its payroll by almost 50,000 people in less than five years. Consider the dramatic reductions in the permanent workforces of the major auto manufacturers during the 1970s, and the steel companies during the 1970s and 1980s. Consider the massive layoffs of middle managers in hundreds of companies that were acquired or merged with others during the acquisition binge of the mid-1980s. Tens of thousands of college-educated managers and professionals who had worked with a company for 5, 10, even 15 or 20 years suddenly found themselves unwanted and expendable cogs in a new company's wheel of fortune. And the process of the post-Industrial Revolution, or whatever name this era comes to be called by, will continue. The new economy does not promise job security for anyone, and any such hope rests on foundations of quicksand.

On the other hand, as a freelance professional, you can lose a client, perhaps your best client, but you always have an opportunity to find new ones. Smart freelancers make finding new clients their first or second priority, practically equal to the importance of keeping current clients happy. You can never be laid off, you can never be fired from a job, and you should never lose your only source of income in any given situation.

It is easy to become complacent if you have one or two important clients who pay well and quickly and provide good, steady work. This, too, is an illusion because any client can suffer reverses and have to abruptly reduce its budget for freelance or consulting work. Accept it; it can, does, and will happen. Yet, by spreading your client base among many companies, you can protect yourself from the worst. You can also develop contingency plans that do not force you to sacrifice your independence. By spreading your risks—which your freelance status enables you to do—you create more and more lasting financial security.

Your Personal Declaration of Independence

Most successful freelancers would never go back to work for a company. Once they taste the fruits of the freelancer's "Tree of Knowledge," they bask in the glow of freedom, and they recognize the opportunities that independence creates, they rightly believe they can never climb back onto the corporate treadmill. For example, a reporter for a newspaper can become an editor, specialize in some aspect of reportage, or shift to another media as a television news reporter or a radio newscaster. The latter path, however, is difficult and rarely taken. Usually, an ambitious reporter seeks to enter newspaper management as an editor or hops from newspaper to newspaper looking for bigger and better assignments. They always work for someone else. They always work the same long days, often 10 to 12 hours under intense pressure, and take orders from perhaps a benign, or perhaps a tyrannical, dictator—their editor. Their salaries are limited to either what a union can get them, or what the market—crowded with reporters willing to work for relatively little—will pay. In one college town, the local newspaper, overwhelmed with job candidates from the college's journalism school, paid its reporters the same starting salary in 1984 that it had paid in 1972—despite the more than doubling of the Consumer Price Index!

Compare the difference between their lot and the prospects that a serious full-time freelance writer has. A freelance writer has the chance to write for thousands of publications about any conceivable subject. From astronomy to accounting, from *Archaeology* to *Family Circle*, a freelance writer is limited only by his or her interests and ability to convince an editor that he or she can deliver the story according to the editor's specifications. This is one aspect only— writing magazine articles—and does not consider freelance public relations work, fiction and creative writing, nonfiction books, freelance copyediting, speechwriting, and dozens of other services a writer can provide.

Even better, if the writer runs into an editor who is a pain in the neck, or a publication that does not pay for six months, a freelance writer can never work with the difficult editor or publication again. Changing jobs just because you do not like the way the boss talks to you is not so easy, and you can get a bad reputation in an industry for "instability." As a freelance professional, you would simply exercise your right to work with the best possible clients and everyone would think you the wiser for your decision.

In short, freelance professionals avoid having just one boss, over whose good and bad characteristics you have no control, and substitute many occasional "bosses" which you more or less have the right to choose. As a freelance professional, you can always say no, turn down offers of work, if you find or believe that the business relationship will not be to your personal or financial benefit. Tell that to your on-the-job superior when he or she gives you an assignment and see what happens!

Time Well Spent

If you are, in theory, free to choose your clients, you are also free to choose how to spend your time. You have the right to choose how you define "success." You can spend the day at the beach and work at night. You can go to the movies in the afternoon when hardly anyone else is there. You can work four hours a day and make

$10,000 a year and be successful, if that is how you define it. Or you can work 16 hours a day, travel around the country meeting with clients, drive yourself to exhaustion, and enjoy making $500,000, or you can think of how to work two hours a day and make $1 million a year. None of these alternatives is impossible or even unreasonable. It depends on what you want to do and how you want to do it.

To a certain extent, of course, this absolute freedom of choice is also an illusion. If you have bills to pay, but no clients, you would act wisely by hustling some work, getting it done, and getting paid for it. If you agree to perform work by a deadline, you do best to meet that deadline, unless serious circumstances—not including spending weeks at the fishing pond or at the movies—prevent it. Your freedom of choice does determine the extent to which you have to actually work. Perhaps for the first time, you will control your lifestyle.

Expressing Yourself

If you choose to freelance in your favorite subject or line of work, you may be able to express yourself and your ideas far more readily, freely, and rewardingly than working for someone else. You can seek out clients who are eager for you to present your ideas and make them succeed. On the other hand, you may see your mission as finding the best ways to serve your clients' requirements. Within the framework of their needs, you can still offer your ideas and stretch your talents and skills, or even learn new skills and exploit latent talents. One latent talent that every successful freelancer quickly discovers he or she has is the ability to sell. If you do not convince, i.e., sell, your clients to buy your services, then you cannot succeed. As we will see in a later chapter, by "selling" we mean the ability to persuade, not the old twist-the-arm, backslapping, shoulder-thumping Willy Loman selling. If you have worked as a manager, or convinced others within an organization to do what you want or think should be done, then you already possess plenty of talent to sell your freelance services.

Freelancing also gives you the chance to explore and exploit talents for which your current job has no use. Perhaps you can sing or play a musical instrument very well. Perhaps you were discouraged as a child from performing professionally, so you have always worked as an engineer. You can hire an agent, accept performing engagements for nights and weekends, and get paid well to do so. You then express that part of yourself that you perhaps had denied in order to work and raise a family.

≪ ACCEPTING THE RISKS ≫

The Biblical analogy of Adam and Eve is appropriate, too, when you consider the risks and drawbacks of professional freelancing. Once Adam and Eve had tasted the fruit of the Tree of Knowledge and they "knew," they suffered the consequences of that knowledge. Similarly, the great rewards of money, freedom of choice, independence, self-expression, and more that freelancing offers are balanced by the often-frightening risks and responsibilities.

Adam and Eve gained knowledge and an incredible world to explore and master when they were driven from the Garden of Eden. But without thinking, they also opened the door to fear, shame, and the loss of innocence. Often, many think that mankind would have been better off if Eve had ignored the snake and Adam had ignored Eve. From this tale—a metaphor for man's coming to consciousness—man gained a universe to explore.

Far less dramatically, when professionals seek the freelance "Tree of Knowledge" by working independently, they find the door to previously unconsidered possibilities opened to them. But they find that they, too, face fear and loss.

In the simplest terms, freelancers may lose time. Part-time freelance professionals, in particular, most often work nights and weekends. They may gain income and reputation, but they lose time with their families. They may lose at least some of their contact with their friends and co-workers.

Their work may cause the loss or upset of family harmony. The time spent away from their families may cause stress and upset. They may bear the brunt of anger and resentments: "You're never at home anymore because of that damn consulting job" or "You never take me anywhere" or "You are ignoring the kids (dog, me, my family, your family, the church, and so on)."

You can ease these negative feelings by discussing your actions long before you take the first step into freelancing. Make sure you and your family understand your goals: "I am working at night so we can buy a new house within two years. I am working on Saturdays and Sundays so you, Jane, can go to that college you want to attend, and you, Johnny, can buy that new sports car you want." Make your purpose clear and keep it foremost in your own and your family's minds. To overcome the feeling of separation, you can establish "sacrosanct" times you will spend with your spouse and family. If you travel a lot, send flowers and love notes. Just do some simple, but caring things to show your family that you are not ignoring them and that you care for and love them.

Yet, spending your evenings and weekends on freelance work can be very difficult and demanding, both emotionally and physically. Get ready for it and the possible negative consequences.

The Buck Stops Here

Many professionals and managers are unfamiliar with the "responsibility of responsibility". You may think, "I supervise 150 people. I know what responsibility means." Yes, to a point. But unless you are the chairman of the board and own all of the stock of the company, you do not carry do-or-die responsibility. A sales manager can blame production or marketing; an engineer can blame sales or production; quality control can blame everybody; and on and on.

As a freelance professional, you have no where to run and no where to hide. You are hired to do a job and perform a very specific task by a certain deadline. If you don't, your inability to perform is laid bare for the client to see. You have to be willing to put your performance on the line every day. Your ability to generate repeat business from satisfied clients depends on your willingness to accept responsibility. You do not have to perform perfectly. If you are wrong or fail to meet a deadline, a client is usually willing to give you the chance to correct the situation, extend a deadline or accommodate some special problem. But you cannot try to blame the client or the client's company, situation, industry, or employees for your shortcoming. You do best and gain the most respect when you forthrightly say, "I was wrong. How can I correct the situation?" That is what the "responsibility of responsibility" really means. Yet many people, long protected by layers of corporate bureaucracy, find this a serious burden which they find difficult to handle.

Unfamiliar and Onerous Tasks

Freelance professionals also face the unpleasant requirement of doing many tasks in which they have little or no training and even less interest. Even if you have an assistant, an accountant, an attorney, an insurance agent, a bookkeeper, a helpful spouse, a hairdresser, a maid, a yardman, a butler, a babysitter, a dog walker, and a cook, you still must do many things as a freelance professional that you never thought you would do and you never wanted to do in the past, or want to do now or in the future. Yet, often, if not every day, you must.

Any freelance professional must, at one time or the other, act as a:

▶ *Collection agency.* If a client holds up payment for 60 or 90 days, and your mortgage is overdue, you will have to call the client's accounts payable department and insist that they pay you. Many people find collecting monies owed for services rendered a very daunting and demeaning task. You usually cannot hire a collection agency to collect for you unless a bill has been past due for months. And if you do, you can assume that you have terminated the relationship with that client. In addition, you will forfeit some portion of the amount collected to the collection agency. Simply complaining about an overdue bill may scare off some clients, but if it does, experience shows that you do not really want those clients in the first place. The author's worst collection experience was with a bill for an article written for the U.S. Department of Education; getting paid took five months of raising Cain, the intervention of a Congressman, and begging a middle level bureaucrat in Washington to authorize a check for just $300. In another case, a freelancer's spouse sat in a client's office and refused to move until she collected a check for a very overdue bill. Despite threats of calling the police, she refused to budge. She got the check, but ended the relationship. However, the freelancer rightly thought, "Who needed it?" Both recalcitrant clients were far more trouble than they were or ever could have been worth to anyone.

▶ *Public relations agent.*   Even if you hire a publicity agent, you still have to toot your own horn. As a freelance of any sort, you cannot hide your light under a bushel and expect clients to spend their time looking for your extraordinary talents and skills hidden under an upside down bushel basket. Contrary to the adage, the world does *not* beat a path to your door simply because you have a better idea. Not a world filled with constant barrages of media clamoring for everyone's time, attention, and dollars!

You must promote your skills, talents, and accomplishments to win freelance work. However, the "pizzazz" with which you present yourself depends on the business. Artists and musicians can do unusual or extraordinary stunts or promotions to gain attention, but an engineer usually should stick with a solid résumé, a list of accomplishments, excellent references from satisfied customers, well-conceived proposals, and good presentations. Usually, without any training or flair for public relations, you have to do most of it yourself. Chapter 7 shows you many appropriate ways to promote your freelance services.

▶ *Customer service representative.* If your client does not like your work, or has a problem, you cannot refer him or her to the customer service department. You have to deal with it and the sooner, the calmer, and the more professional, the better. If you do not like criticism (who does?), at least learn to accept it graciously.

▶ *Financial planner.* Some freelance professionals, such as media stars and celebrities, can afford the services of a top-notch financial planner or business manager. Most freelance professionals cannot afford to do so and must manage their own finances. If you managed finances badly while you were working, you are even more likely to manage badly when you freelance. You will need a good CPA to do your income tax returns at least once a year and preferably once a quarter. You may want to hire a freelance bookkeeper to come in once a month and pay your bills and balance, however precariously, your books. Many freelance professionals who cannot afford these regular services, must cope on their own with an often frustrating and—we hope—an at least as often exhilarating task. If you do not have a head for numbers, plan a sensible alternative.

▶ *Salesperson.* Just as you must publicize your efforts and promote yourself, you must also sell your services. Most importantly, successful selling means knowing how to *close* a sale. Many freelancers know how to give good presentations because they have worked in project management or similar positions. But you may not be familiar with the necessity—and the difficulty—of asking someone to "buy" you and the services you offer. The willingness to simply ask for the business, however haltingly or badly you do it at first, makes the single most important difference between success and failure. Why? Very few clients will come out of the woodwork and ask you to work for them. Many clients will come to you from referrals and want to consider your credentials. You must still persuade them of your superiority and ask them to buy your service. A simple "When can we start?" or "Can we do business together?" or "How can I help you?" will do at first. As you gain experience, you can learn more sophisticated selling techniques. But start somewhere and always ask for the sale.

In the best of times, in freelancing professional services, closing a sale takes shape as a meeting of the minds. The client and you work toward a mutual understanding of what that client requires and how your services will fulfill those needs. In the real world, you will spend a lot of time helping a client recognize and quantify exactly how his or her requirements should be defined. Then, you show the client how you can help fulfill those requirements, solve problems, or improve situations. On other occasions, you may spend most of your time overcoming the client's fear of contracting with you, not because you cannot do the job or the job does not need to be done, but because the client fears losing his or her job or losing face with the boss, or refuses to contemplate the real nature of the situation. As you may know already, managers and executives make emotional decisions as often as everyone else, and you have to know how to cope with, if not capitalize on, those emotions.

▶ *"Investor" relations.* This is a complex corporate function which translates, in the freelancer's world, into a simple task: Making the bank happy. You need to establish and maintain a strong relationship with a local bank. If you borrow money from a bank, it essentially takes a share of your profits, for example, when you make loan payments, the bank assumes an informal equity interest in your business. If the bank requires collateral or security against your equipment or business assets, it takes a formal interest in your business just as much as a partner or stockholder. Keeping a good record of deposits and withdrawals, showing a steadily increasing income and establishing a personal relationship with the branch manager, vice president, or key personal banker will help you obtain loans, and extra consideration if you face a financial crisis. Freelancers often experience peaks and valleys in getting paid; short-term (less than a year) loans from a cooperative bank will go far to smooth out any rough spots on the road to success.

It is easier to establish such a relationship with a small, community bank that depends on the good will of local businesspeople for its success. If you share your success with them by keeping large balances, going to them for home mortgages, car loans and the like, you will become a valued customer. If you gain a wide reputation, or even a bit of celebrity, the bankers will even enjoy having you as a customer. If you publish a book, give your banker a signed copy; if you write an article, and it has a "nugget" of interest, send the banker a copy. Send a meaningful present during the winter holidays. These little extra signs of appreciation go far toward gaining the bankers' extraordinary cooperation when you need it.

Ostensibly, none of these tasks have anything to do with the actual work you do. But you will often find to your chagrin that you spend more time on them than you spend doing the actual work you get paid to do.

The Terrors

Perhaps the single greatest and certainly most demanding problem is what the author calls "the terrors." The complete responsibility, the frequent isolation of working alone, the peaks and valleys of getting paid, the frustration of losing a good client or not "landing" a good prospect, the fear of failure or the fear of success all can conspire in your head to create emotional turmoil, if not occasional panic. It appears that every freelancer, even those with more than adequate cash in the bank, experience the terrors at least a few times as they get started.

You can cope with the terrors in many ways, but with one principle: Believe in yourself and what you are doing. Some people cope by working harder to relieve their sense that they are not doing enough to succeed. Others take a break and use stress reduction techniques to slow their heart rate and calm down. The terrors may last a minute or two, or they can last for hours. The essential action to *avoid* during the terrors is making a decision to quit. Put off any decisions. If you do make a hasty decision, keep in the back of your mind that you have the right, when you feel more relaxed and calm, to reverse any decision made in a moment of panic.

In short, expect the terrors to strike—and combat them with faith in your mission and your goals.

In spite of all of these risks and unsought responsibilities, most freelance professionals find it very difficult, usually impossible, to go back to a regular job after they experience a modicum of success. The freedom, the feeling of control, the increased income and the sense of accomplishment that "here is something I can truly call my own" more than compensate for the fears and risks. Yet, some people just do not have the physical, emotional or psychological make-up to succeed as a freelance professional. In the next chapter, we discuss how you can determine whether or not you have what it takes to succeed on your own.

≪ 2 ≫

SHOULD YOU FREELANCE?

≪ THE FREELANCE MINDSET ≫

Serious, full-time freelancers have a definite mindset, an attitude that their work is for keeps. They believe deeply and act accordingly that their freelance status is permanent. They turn down good jobs when offered them. They discourage, to say the least, clients that want to turn a freelance relationship into a boss/subordinate one.

You can easily separate serious freelancers from the many people who only think they want to work as a freelance professional. Offer them the prospect of a good job that perhaps even pays better and gives them a better title than what they had in their last job. If they jump at the chance to take that job, they were always biding their time. In the back of their minds, they may have always believed that they were "just between jobs." Serious freelancers value their freedom and their opportunity more than the promise of a little more money and a little better pay. The author has turned down five excellent job offers simply because he enjoys his freedom. When you work as a freelancer, turn down your first job offer, and then say to yourself, "Am I glad I didn't take that job!" then you will know you have crossed the freelance Rubicon never to turn back.

Of course, serious circumstances, such as a life-threatening illness in the family, dire financial need and the like, can compel even a committed freelancer to look for and accept a new job.

Part-Timers Are Different

Part-time freelancers usually have different mindsets. They have short-term personal, financial, or career goals that they want to reach. They do not consider their freelance activities as ends in themselves, but as temporary means to short-term ends. Some part-timers use freelancing as a way to gradually build a nest egg and a reputation so they can eventually wean themselves away from the corporate nest or prepare for an early retirement.

Either full-time or part-time freelancing is a legitimate activity, but this chapter is more oriented to the person who wants to become a serious, full-time freelance professional. Chapter 4 will help both part-timers and full-timers get started, but most of the emotional, family, professional, and business influences that determine whether or not you should freelance do not apply to part-timer freelancers. Of course, part-timers face stresses and strains, such as time away from their families, but they do not need to develop the complete and all important break with the "job" mentality that full-timers must make to succeed happily.

≪ PERSONAL INFLUENCES ≫

As a grain of sand irritates an oyster to grow a pearl, every person who becomes a freelancer first confronts frustration and then becomes so irritated with the source of that frustration that he or she takes action. A person satisfied with his or her place in the corporate hierarchy, someone who wants to become president of the company more than anything else, simply will not experience or feel the kind of frustration that drives a person to become a freelancer. To answer the question posed in the title of this chapter, "Should you freelance?", you need to identify the sources of frustration in your professional and personal life.

Very often, you are stymied in your job. Perhaps you were overlooked for a promotion. Perhaps you are stuck on the middle rungs of the ladder to the top of your corporation and your prospects with another company would be even worse or your goals more difficult to reach. Perhaps you are convinced that your superiors are incompetent and that you could do the job much better. Perhaps you identify a market for a service, but your company is not interested in exploiting the opportunity because potential revenues are too small for the company to consider.

Regardless of the source or combination of sources of your frustration, you strongly believe that you, acting alone or in concert with just a few others, could do the job better, make more money, and accrue more benefits than others within a usual corporate structure. Basically, you have an "I can do it better" attitude and you are determined to prove it.

Revenge as a Positive Motive

Revenge is often criticized as a negative, disabling motivator that prevents people from succeeding in the long term. This is not always the case. Revenge often acts as the primer cap that explodes the dynamite of freelance success. However, revenge works best if you channel your revengeful and angry thoughts into positive channels. Thinking "I'll show the jerks" can motivate you to become a freelancer far more quickly than any deliberate plan. The problem arises when you, in fact, have shown the jerks. What do you do now? If you have not replaced revenge as a motive with a positive attitude toward continuing your success, revenge can turn very sour indeed. You simply run out of steam. You exhaust your emotional energy and you are left with no compelling reason to continue.

But if you do change your angry attitude into positive striving to achieve, revenge can indeed by sweet. If you succeed, your former

tormentors will certainly know about it and perhaps envy your freedom, success, reputation, and prosperity. Remember, too, that living well is the best revenge, and by and large, successful freelancers
live far better than their corporate counterparts.

≪ POSITIVE FRUSTRATIONS ≫

Healthy frustration can also come from positive sources. Perhaps
you often get requests from your co-workers to share your knowledge and skills. Professional journals and magazines ask you to
write articles. Professional societies ask you to sit on or chair committees, coordinate conferences, sit on discussion panels and industry forums. Universities ask you to be a guest lecturer. You enjoy
giving seminars, teaching college students, or leading or participating in conferences and forums, but you do not have the time to
devote to these activities because your job demands most of your
available time.

Perhaps you have a strong and respected reputation in your
field. You know you have much to offer your industry, but your job
prevents you from sharing as much of your knowledge or expand-
ing your horizons as much as you would like. These circumstances
can act as powerful and positive motivators to freelance. Successful
consultants have long known that sitting on panels at trade shows,
participating in conferences, giving papers, writing for professional
journals, and the like help generate new business. A good reputation makes it much easier to sign up clients.

If you experience either positive or negative frustrations, or
both, and you find yourself unwilling to tolerate them any longer,
you have taken a major step toward a freelance career.

≪ ANALYZE PERSONAL GOALS ≫

When you consider freelancing, write a short, concise personal
"mission statement." This is a buzzword in current business jargon,
but it can have a great impact on your thinking. Many companies

prepare mission statements or determine their mission in order to focus everyone's efforts in one direction—toward accomplishing that mission. You need a similar statement for your freelance work. You may not think of working freelance as a business, but quickly disabuse yourself of the notion that freelancing is something other than a business. Your purpose is to provide clients with a "product," in this case, your services. You seek to get paid for providing that product and you want to show a profit after you subtract the expenses of the endeavor. That is one of the classic definitions of a business. You need a mission statement for the same reason a billion-dollar company does: To establish a focus for your efforts.

This statement will also help you determine whether or not you should freelance. When you write your statement, include your one-, five- and ten-year goals. Put down what you would do if you could do anything in your profession or field. If you write down statements such as "Within five years, I want to be president of a $500 million food service company," or "As the pinnacle of my career, I want to be head of the leading electronic engineering laboratory in the automotive industry," then you should question your commitment to working freelance, unless doing that for a few years can help you attain your long-term goals. But most freelance work will do little to help a person who wants to succeed within an organizational environment.

A mission statement or long-term goal such as "Within ten years, I want to own the largest firm of consulting civil engineers in New York City," or "Within ten years, I want to be semi-retired with an independent income" indicates a much stronger commitment to the freelance life.

Of course, many people do not begin with such clear-cut and strong commitments. As they work freelance part-time, they see how the advantages can overshadow the drawbacks, and their commitment to a full-time freelance career evolves into something deep, broad, and permanent. Clearly, successful freelancers are neither sitting by the phone waiting for a job offer, nor walking the pavements looking for a job. They recognize that they not only have demanding work, they have a demanding career and a new, vastly preferable lifestyle. They understand that their freelance activities will shape their futures. Freelancing becomes their most important and most permanent business commitment.

≪ THINK THROUGH FAMILY INFLUENCES ≫

After your professional situation, the most important influence will be your family's attitudes. This was briefly mentioned in Chapter 1, but their attitudes become essential when you answer the question that this chapter poses.

If you want to freelance to satisfy family financial needs, first consider whether or not there are other ways you can meet those needs? Would you rather change jobs and get a raise or a promotion? Can you get a raise or promotion, change departments, accept relocation, or work overtime and satisfy yourself and the family's need for money more easily than you can start your own freelance business? If the answer is yes to any of these or similar questions, then try these steps first before you freelance. You are not ready to take the great leap.

Next, you should discuss freelancing with your spouse and older children. Do you have their wholehearted support? Do they understand that they may have to make short-term sacrifices until your freelance work brings in the desired higher income? Do they give signs or say that they will feel overly burdened or abandoned if you take this step? You may explain to them that you want to freelance so you can give them what they want, yet they may still not understand. Look for signs that they do not really hear or understand your goals. They may not always be direct.

If your spouse works, is he or she willing to provide short-term cash requirements to pay the bills? Is he or she willing to spend some of your savings, cash in some of your investments, take out a second mortgage on the house, or take similar steps to help you get started? If the answer is an adamant "No!", then you, as a family, are not ready for this change. You need to persuade your spouse of the fundamental wisdom of your action. You can also take steps over a period of months to provide enough working capital so you and your family do not suffer undue hardship. Frankly, most freelancers do not take this precaution, however wise and thoughtful it is, and it may be their single worst mistake, as will be explained in detail in Chapter 4.

Are you prepared for arguments that arise from your own or your family's fear of loss? The core of most arguments about freelancing appears to be insecurity—personal, financial, or family. Can you cope with these insecurities and anxieties and act as, if not a pillar of strength, at least as the glue that holds the family together? Can you patiently, yet persistently work through these problems, yet continue to get your work done? You must be able to honestly answer "yes" to these questions, or you may face a very difficult and deteriorating family situation.

Succeeding as a freelancer when the family has serious apprehensions or even actively opposes the idea will be very difficult. You need to discuss beforehand possible changes in living habits and lifestyle for you and your family. Many of these issues will be discussed later in this chapter. You need to be sensitive to your family's concerns, but you also need to emphasize the advantages and opportunities you seek. In fact, you need to explain how taking this step will make you happy and bring you more fulfillment in your work and in your life. It may well be that if you have been unhappy and dissatisfied in your work, your family may heartily endorse a change. Your family may be more aware than you know of your frustration and unhappiness. You may knowingly or unconsciously let your feelings and frustration show in anger, depression, withdrawal, or uncooperativeness. Your family may welcome the chance for you to feel happiness and express positive emotions again.

More than likely, if you are happy about going freelance, your family will be happy that you are doing what you most want to do. The benefits that count the most for them may not be the new house or the vacations, but your sharing of your happiness with them.

≪ FACE THE EMOTIONAL IMPACT ≫

In the previous chapter, some of the compelling emotional issues were addressed as drawbacks. You should fully consider them and most importantly your reaction to them before you decide to freelance.

Personal Involvement and Separation

One of a job's appealing aspects is that usually you can leave the office at 5 P.M. and forget about it until the next day. If you are a 9-to-5er, who can or *wants* to forget about the job until the next morning, you may have a hard time as a freelancer. A freelance career tends to become much of your life. You think about it in the shower, you worry about it on vacation, you talk about it when you go out to lunch with your spouse, you keep it in the back of your mind all of the time for one simple reason: You are the business. Of course, you should not become obsessed or compulsive and worry so much that you become unable to work or lose sleep. Rather, since you are directly responsible for your success or failure, you have a far more active concern than if you were an office worker or one professional in a department of many. The success or failure of a corporate enterprise does not usually depend on your work; that of your freelance business does.

Yet, you also need the ability to analyze events objectively. Separating yourself from your decisions and an honest analysis of your business situation requires a lot of self-esteem, but not "ego," in the negative sense of the word. You need to be critical of your actions, and willing to change directions, yet not succumb to self-condemnation. Can you think, "Oh damn. I blew that one. What do I have to do to better approach the next potential client?" instead of "Oh damn. I blew that one. I'll never get another client again as long as I live. That was one of the most idiotic things anyone has ever done." This example is only slightly exaggerated.

Handling Rejection

In fact, confronting rejection and turning it into opportunity is probably the single greatest emotional challenge a freelancer faces. Salespeople are usually taught how to handle rejection and how to avoid turning it into paralyzing fear. Most freelance professionals do not have this experience, and many have never suffered frequent rejection. Yet, freelance professionals must expect to have most of their proposals and presentations rejected. They face being turned down by as many as nine out of ten of their potential clients. Even when you have a client, you face the possibility that the client will dislike your presentation, ignore your recommendations, and never hire you again. Even when a client accepts most of a report, survey or presentation, he or she may still want it modified, pick at the niggliest of details and force you to redo it several times. Yet, as much as you may feel like telling the client to go jump into the proverbial lake, you almost certainly will need the patience and fortitude to accept their criticisms, rework the job, and present it again, with if not a smile on your face, then at least an active willingness to cooperate.

Persistence Pays

The best way to handle rejection is with persistence. It is like overcoming your fear as a child after you fall off a bicycle; the cure is to get back on the bicycle and try again. Salespeople well know that the best way to deal with rejection or a lost sale is to immediately make another sales call. Most sales experts agree—and most successful freelancers would, too—that selling is a numbers game. The more sales calls you make the more likely you are to find a buyer. The same principle holds true in any freelance endeavor. If you call a dozen potential clients, send out 50 solicitations or proposals, and knock on 25 doors, all to no avail, you must be willing, when you know you'd rather give up and go to a movie, to make one more phone call, send out one more proposal, and knock on one more door. Persistence pays not only in successfully signing up new clients, but in overcoming the negative emotions, the letdown and feelings of worthlessness that rejection can cause.

You practice persistence in several ways. You can let fear motivate you to keep calling; you can rely on a strong belief in yourself or your mission; you can promise yourself a reward at the end of the day, a project, or an arbitrary period if you persist and succeed. In short, you promise yourself future rewards for short-term sacrifices.

If you truly know that you handle rejection badly, you can do one of two things:

1. Reconsider the idea of freelancing.
2. Learn to turn rejection into opportunity.

With a solid self-esteem, you can say to yourself, "So, the jerk doesn't like my work. Okay. That's his opinion. I know it is good, even excellent, and I'll make sure that that guy's competitor gets a chance to take full advantage of it."

You don't learn to *like* rejection. That's self-destructive. Learn to convert your negative feelings into positive actions. But if you have a serious need for the constant approval of others, succeeding as a freelancer may prove difficult. On the other hand, a modicum of needing approval enables you to work well with clients. After all, you do need their approval of your ideas and services to succeed; try to avoid confusing that need with an unhealthy personal need for approval of your "self," or constant support for a fragile ego.

Handling a Dependence on Others

If you really enjoy the camaraderie of working in an office environment with many people around all day, you may need to reconsider freelancing. Freelancers of every sort spend many hours alone or isolated, even when they work with assistants or their spouses. The feeling of aloneness also derives from a sense and the reality of responsibility.

You must be able to accept a task, assemble all of the scattered resources needed to execute that task, and then do it, often alone or with relatively little assistance. You may spend many hours alone in libraries or research facilities. You may spend many nights alone in hotel rooms if your work requires that you travel. You may spend hours each day or week preparing reports, doing spreadsheets on personal computers, or working with word processors or type-writers. You may spend hours each day or week in your car, on air-planes or on public transportation.

You must consider whether or not you can tolerate, and if not like, at least make productive use of all of this time alone. If you truly enjoy the proverbial bull sessions in an office, or congregat-ing around the coffee machine, or lunch in the cafeteria with your peers, think again. Freelancing can be a lonely business.

Handling Subordinate Relationships

Even if you do have a lot of contact with other people, much of that contact will be in somewhat subordinate relationships. The client is the boss, and you must work to satisfy that client's needs even when you disagree with the client's decisions. Of course, you can drop that client, but freelancers find few clients who will do things en-tirely their way all or even most of the time. If you are used to being the boss, or have many years experience as a manager, you must be prepared to be the subordinate, or at best, the equal in a client-to-advisor relationship.

You also face many hours of relatively artificial contact with other people. You may spend hours on the phone interviewing prospects, discussing projects with clients, gathering information for a project, and so forth. Most of these, you hope, will be pleasant and produc-tive business discussions, but they are unlikely to result in the same kind or quality of friendships many people make when they work in offices around many other people.

On the other hand, you may find that you get to know different, if not much more interesting friends among your clients or contacts. If your circle of friends had been limited to co-workers within your department, you now have the chance, governed by the available time, to cultivate acquaintances and friends from an entire industry. You often associate with the very best people in your field, an opportunity you may never have had in your job. You can explore different fields, and as an expert in one, call on experts in the others either for business purposes or simply because you want to. For example, the author has developed an interest in the ancient history of a foreign country, and his work for the government of that country has enabled him to meet leading historians and archaeologists and discuss his personal interest with them. Freelancing gives you the chance to create similar situations for any of your professional or personal interests.

Your family can also benefit from new and varied experiences. The author's work has enabled his nephew to take rarely allowed tours of fireboats, meet leading figures in news broadcasting, meet major league baseball players, travel extensively, and meet leading figures in sports writing, the nephew's intended career. These opportunities for young family members to have fascinating and unusual experiences are not limited to freelancers, of course, but arranging them can become much easier. Most important of all, these experiences may open up new possibilities to children and young people so they can understand that they have the chance to excel, the chance to avoid the normal career paths, the chance to develop their potential in ways they could never have considered before.

Changing Relationships

If you work for your previous employer as a consultant, prepare for the relationship between your former co-workers, subordinates and superiors to change, often dramatically. Many people will accept your new relationship, but others may use it to make your freelance work difficult to complete. They may subtly or overtly interfere with your project. Since you are not in the office every day to defend yourself, your former opponents within the company may very well spread rumors, gossip about you when you are not around, and look for ways to criticize your performance as a freelancer. You will need to maintain and strengthen the support of your former superiors, and you should be prepared to give your former employer the best quality work you can provide. In freelancing, distance does not make the corporate heart grow fonder. "Out of sight, out of mind" is more likely the correct adage about which to be concerned.

≪ COPING WITH THE NEED FOR DISCIPLINE ≫

New freelancers often experience a temporary sense of euphoria. Many revel in their new freedom, and, at first, may tend to overdo it. They putter in the garden, have lunch with business associates without a business purpose, in short, they waste time as they exult in their new freedom. Perhaps the most important lifestyle issue you face is old-fashioned discipline. To succeed as a freelancer, you must quickly and relatively efficiently create a new routine for yourself. You need to establish new work habits that enable you to sign up new clients, serve the needs of active clients—with quality work delivered on time—collect monies owed, pay your bills, and still have some time for yourself and your family.

The temptations to avoid working according to a disciplined routine are legion. A working spouse may now think that you have nothing better to do than to take the kids to school, do the grocery shopping, clean up the house, mow the lawn, etc. You may get "hooked" on soap operas or sports events; today, most cable television systems offer dozens of channels and there may be several shows on during working hours that you could tell yourself that you "just have to watch." (Get a VCR and tape them for viewing after your work for the day is completed.) In short, as a freelancer, especially if you work at home, distractions are a major pitfall. And if you work alone, it can become quite lonely, so you could start "drinking" lunch at the corner bar, or finding excuses to run errands when you should be working.

Using Inexpensive Executive Office Space

This need for a disciplined environment is why many freelance professionals rent office space. The popularity of "executive offices" which provide furniture, assistants, office machines, telephone answering services, and so on, demonstrates both how many people today work freelance, and how many people find it very difficult to work effectively at home.

Executive offices are very easy to find in any city, especially in new commercial buildings. Usually, a developer will divide a floor into many small offices with a central reception and telephone switchboard. A room for copiers, facsimile machines, mailing machines, and other office equipment will be set aside, and you can use them for a monthly fee or on a per-use basis. Look in the real estate classified advertisements in your local newspaper or business journal under headings like "executive offices" to find these offices in your area.

Monthly rental costs for executive offices depend on the amount of space you want, whether you want to sign a lease, and local demand. Office sizes range from 10 feet by 12 feet to suites of five or six connected rooms. Prices range from as low as $200 per month for one office to several thousand dollars a month for suites. In South Florida, for example, depending on location, one-room executive offices rent for $250 to $395 per month.

The worst problem with this method of renting space is the extra charges you may have to pay. Usually, the only "free" services which a developer offers include a receptionist, office furniture, someone to answer your business telephone line, conference rooms, mail handling service, and the like. But you usually have to pay extra for secretarial services, use of photocopiers and other equipment, postage and so forth. In addition, you will have to pay a higher business rate for your telephone and the very high installation costs to the local telephone company. You need to carefully consider whether you can work out of your home efficiently and avoid these additional, often substantial, costs.

Renting an executive office may or may not bring you the prestige you desire as well. Two schools of thought enter into this: One holds that any business address is better than either working out of your home, an answering machine, or a mail box address; the second holds that clients will not give any more credence to your freelance status if they visit you in an executive office. It may show some clients that you cannot afford an assistant; it may tell others that you are smart to rent office services as economically as possible. It depends, too, on whether you primarily do freelance work with established clients who don't care whether or not you live in Timbuktu, or new clients who need to be reassured of your *bona fides* as a serious business person. If the latter, consider executive office space.

But renting an executive office does not mean that you have to create your own 9-to-5 rut. You probably started freelancing to get out of that rut. Rather, you need enough discipline to accomplish your goals. If you want to write the next bestselling novel within a year or two, you have to sit at the keyboard and write chapters to do it. The late mystery writer Rex Stout never spent more than 38 days on any of his novels, but Robert Ludlum spends hours a day writing in longhand and correcting drafts that his assistant types. You may not want to be a novelist, but the point is the same regardless of your field. The discipline you practice depends directly on what you wish to accomplish, how much money you want to make, and how quickly you want to reach those goals.

≪ ARE YOU READY TO FREELANCE? ≫

Ten Essential Questions to Find the Answer

This is not a quiz in which there are clearcut answers. Each question has four answers, labeled A to D. The A answers indicate a strong likelihood that you would succeed as a freelance professional; the B answers indicate a good likelihood that you can improve this situation and succeed; the C answers indicate a weakness; and D answers strongly indicate you will have a problem with this situation if you decide to freelance. At the end of the questionnaire, add up the answers for each letter. For example, you may have two As, one B, three Cs and four Ds. A total of predominantly Cs and Ds, such as this, would indicate that you should consider long and hard before you decide to freelance. In this example, the negatives clearly outweigh the positives. On the other hand, if your answers are predominantly As and Bs, you have a very good chance to succeed.

Question 1: Does your spouse support your decision to freelance?

   A. Yes, he is an enthusiastic and strong supporter.

   B. Yes, but he is concerned about the lack of a steady income.

   C. No, but he will work with me for six months to a year to help make my decision work.

   D. No, he is adamant that the idea will not work.

Question 2: Do you enjoy working on many projects at the same time without direct supervision from others?

   A. Yes, they get my creative juices flowing and I prefer to work at my own pace.

   B. Yes, but I prefer to restrict my workload to only a few things at a time.

   C. Somewhat, but I know I can only finish one thing at a time.

   D. No, I really prefer to work with direct supervision most of the time.

Question 3: In a corporate situation, were you ever considered a maverick, but a maverick that got things done?

   A. Yes, I was often alone in my recommendations and ideas.

   B. Yes, to a point, and only when I strongly believed in my ideas.

C. No, but I could occasionally see where the real mavericks were right.

D. No, I usually think that company executives develop policies for the best of all concerned.

Question 4: Do you enjoy meeting the needs of clients, even if those needs conflict with what you think is best?

A. Yes, my mission is to serve my client's needs as we both understand them.

B. Yes, but when I think I am correct, I fight hard for my recommendations.

C. No, not as a rule, but I am willing to consider what they want.

D. No, why would they hire me as a freelance if they wanted it done their way in the first place?

Question 5: Do you want to work independently during the rest of your career?

A. Yes, I can think of nothing I would rather do.

B. Yes, but I would like to establish a firm of professionals in the same field and build a prominent consulting business.

C. No, I would take a job again, but I want to try freelancing for awhile.

D. No, I prefer to work for a company, but I have to act as a consultant while I am between jobs.

Question 6: Do you almost always accept responsibility for your own actions?

A. Yes, I know that I usually cause what happens to me, good or bad.

B. Yes, but sometimes, circumstances beyond my control make others responsible for the results.

C. Somewhat, but more often than not, I have little influence over what happens.

D. Occasionally, but what others do to me gives my actions little meaning.

Question 7: Can you accept the possibility of short-term financial insecurity?

A. Yes, I know that the potential financial gain I can make as a freelancer far outstrips any short-term financial problems.

B. Yes, but I need to make sure I have a solid financial foundation before I start freelancing.

C. Perhaps, but I would prefer that at least one family member receives a regular paycheck for as long as I continue to freelance.

D. No, I strongly prefer to have a regular paycheck.

Question 8: Do you enjoy taking risks, that is, are you willing to put your time, energy, brainpower and experience on the line in the open marketplace?

A. Yes, freelancing is the opportunity I've been waiting for to express my ideas that have been stymied for so long.

B. Yes, but I try to make sure that I have carefully prepared to take on the risks.

C. Perhaps, but I prefer to reduce the risks as much as possible before I take action.

D. No, I prefer to work under the guidance and direction of others and let them decide which risks to take.

Question 9: Do you deal well with the picky details of your work?

A. Yes, I usually stay on top of the details involved in each project.

B. Yes, but I may need an assistant to help manage the load.

C. Not really, and I need someone else to help keep things straight.

D. No, I always feel overwhelmed if I have to deal with details.

Question 10: Do you like to show or teach other people how they can improve their situations?

A. Yes, I believe that I am an excellent teacher and I bring positive attributes to any business situation.

B. Yes, I like to share my knowledge and experience as well as I can.

C. Not usually, I'll help someone understand a situation if I am asked and I know the answer.

D. No, I would make a terrible teacher or instructor.

« 3 »

HAVE YOU GOT
WHAT IT TAKES?

One of potential freelancers' greatest fears is that they are not qualified for what they want to do. They worry that unless they show a client a booklength résumé of positions held and goals accomplished, they will not receive work from their clients. The purpose of this chapter is to ease those concerns. In almost all of the freelance fields considered in this book, you need no more than the basic education and training and solid work experience required of any competent professional.

For example, if you wish to work as a freelance bookkeeper, you need either several years of active, recent experience, or a community college degree and some work experience. Of course, if a profession requires more stringent training to achieve a basic, acceptable status, then you have to have that training and those qualifications. A computer systems analyst needs a degree in the field and several years of successful experience working on the specific types of mainframe computers that his clients operate. An attorney working freelance for a bank must have a law degree, with a specialty in banking and corporate law.

Not only do some fields require you to attain a higher education, your potential clients may not consider you adequately informed enough to help them, if you do not have academic and working credentials at least similar to, if not superior to, their own. Scientific and engineering clients can be very emphatic about academic credentials.

One advantage a freelancer has is the "aura" of the outside expert. Education, skills, and experience can enhance that aura and make working with clients easier. If you have more qualifications than they do, they may be more willing to accept your recommendations or agree with your point of view.

≪ "DEGREES" OF DIFFICULTY ≫

The following degrees from advanced or accredited educational institutions should be considered the minimum level of education that you should have attained before you freelance in each field. In some cases, such as a fiction writer, it is not necessary to have a college degree, but educational attainment of some kind tends to impress clients more than lack of education.

Let's consider various types of degrees and some freelance fields for which each type is appropriate.

▶ *Associate of arts.*   Or community college, vocational education, or technical school degrees. They would be appropriate for certain types of freelance work, including bookkeepers, computer repair technicians, entry-level programmers, commercial artists, paste-up and layout artists, personal teaching and instructors (from music to exercise classes), court reporters, paralegal assistants, home health aides, editorial proofreaders, and typesetters.

▶ *Bachelor's degrees.*   With the exception of the licensed professions and the academic fields, a bachelor's degree and solid work experience provides more than adequate qualifications for many freelance fields including: editor, marketing consultant, management consultant, accountant, financial planner, advertising copywriter, public relations counsel, interior designer (those without the ASID—American Society of Interior Design—certification), photographers, broadcasters, systems analysts, business school instructors, attorneys, architects, child guidance and development counselors, and so forth.

▶ *Master's degrees.* In technical and scientific fields, a master's degree, with advanced work and attendance at many symposia and seminars is generally required. All kinds of consulting engineers, consulting chemists, environmental management consultants, urban planners, and the like tend to have master's degrees or better. Very well-known and experienced people can succeed with just a bachelor's. Management consultants or specialists in various financial fields may need MBAs (masters of business administration).

▶ *Licensed professions and related degrees.* These include licensed practical nurses, registered nurses, attorneys, certified public accountants, and psychologists (in some states).

▶ *Doctorates.* Only in highly specialized research or academic freelance work will you need a doctorate or degrees beyond a master's. In fact, a doctorate may, in many fields, make you over qualified. You can price yourself out of the market. For example, a freelance artist has no need for a doctorate, but an independent child guidance counselor certainly needs a master's and a doctorate may impress his or her potential clients. Of course, if you primarily work as a college professor or in a top research position within a corporation, your doctorate is a job requirement, and clients for your freelance work would expect you to have those credentials.

▶ *Professional certification.* Many freelance professions also either require or definitely benefit from professional certifications. A financial planner or insurance underwriter should have a Certified Life Underwriter (CLU) or Certified Financial Planner (CFP) certification to be able to offer clients the knowledge they need to make successful financial decisions. The same goes for accountants, of course, who could have CPAs. Management consultants can earn the status of Certified Management Accountant (CMA) by attending seminars and combining these credits with work experience.

▶ *No degrees required.* Fortunately, for many freelance professions, degrees in the field are not required. Artists, writers—especially fiction writers—exercise and physical fitness instructors, photographers, home inspectors, skin divers, tour and travel guides, yacht brokers, charter boat captains and crews, proofreaders, and more do not need degrees.

It may impress potential clients more if you have a professional certificate, or, in some cases, have studied at well-known schools. An artist, for example, may have studied at the Art Students League in New York City; it does not grant degrees, but its instructors are among the best artists in the world. People in the art world would know an artist received quality instruction if he or she had studied at this school. An aerobics instructor may have more knowledge that can help his or her clients if he or she has studied physical education. A natural foods nutritionist may study at various schools of natural health without obtaining a degree, yet still be well qualified to advise clients on how to eat more healthfully and wisely.

≪ WORK QUALITY STILL MOST IMPORTANT ≫

However, degrees and certifications only show clients that you have the basic knowledge they need to get the job done. In most cases, you can still overcome the lack of an advanced degree that most freelancers or professionals in your field have with years of quality experience and by performing quality work. Equally, you can lose clients by delivering poor quality work regardless of the number of degrees you have. Clients may hire you on the basis of a degree, but, as they have the right to do, they will demand results. Your degree will not carry any weight in pleasing the client if you don't deliver quality work.

The Specialty Problem

Another serious consideration you must face is the "generalist versus specialist" problem. Of course, if you need brain surgery, you don't hire a podiatrist. But many clients believe they need specialists and look long and hard for them when they only need a well-qualified generalist.

For example, a food processing company may need a management consultant to do a survey on internal procedures. The executive in charge may feel compelled to find a management consultant with deep experience in the food industry, in other words, a specialist. But in many cases, a qualified management consultant with experience in similar raw materials processing industries can do the job just as well, if not better. Consultants in the food processing industry, however, may encourage the executive to hold onto his beliefs so they can continue to monopolize the freelance work that the company needs.

One answer for the beleaguered generalist with experience and interests that cover many fields is this: Pretend to be a specialist. Design what could be called a "Chinese Restaurant Menu" résumé: from the entire "menu" of your background, training, degrees and experience, take one "order" of experience from Column A, take another "order" of training from Column B, and another "order" of background from the *á la carte* side of the menu. Put them together into a résumé or *vita* specifically targeted to the client's requirements.

Is this deceitful or dishonest? No, the client does not care whether you can speak Swahili, if he wants to hire you to reorganize his marketing department. So, you merely confuse a client if you dump everything you have ever done in his lap.

For example, the author has written books about everything from personal computers to Social Security to franchising to selling techniques to this one on freelancing. His experience shows that when he shows editors everything he has written, many respond, "But have you ever written about _____." Fill in the blank with the specific topic with which the editors are immediately concerned.

The client is, very rightly, interested only in whether or not you can do the job he needs done. To save your time and make the client's task easier, you, as a generalist, should provide the client with the information directly related to that need.

What if you do not have the background, experience, or training directly related to the client's need, but you know you can perform the task and do it well? Draw on and emphasize the most closely related experiences you have. Then impress the client with your versatility to prove that you can easily learn what you do not know and apply your indirect experience to succeed at the task.

You can also impress new clients with your credentials, degrees, and background that are superior to those required for the task at hand. For example, a new freelance advertising copywriter had written several business books, but had not written any advertising copy since some freelance assignments early in her career. Yet, she convinced the director of an advertising agency to let her write advertising copy at a high rate of pay because he was very impressed that he would have a published author doing the work. (Giving him and his wife autographed copies of her books also helped prove the person's skills and promote her status, but the point is the same.) The client thinks—and may actually be—getting more talent, skill, and experience than he originally thought he would. If he gains the benefits of the superior experience, talent, and skill at the price he wanted to pay or could afford, the client will rightly feel that he is getting a bargain.

Why would someone with superior experience accept work that demands less? Three very good reasons: First, money or the need for it; second, relatively easy work that makes smooth the peaks and valleys between more difficult projects; and third, a strong desire to gain experience in a relatively new or different field. The new copywriter had tired of writing books and saw that advertising offered a new, exciting, and potentially more profitable challenge than writing business books. The hectic, results-oriented pace of advertising reminded her of her early work as a newspaper reporter, but advertising had two advantages over newspaper work. It was far more lucrative; and advertising's whole purpose was to sell, a far more honorable pursuit, she believed, than chasing police cars and prying into people's lives to report the "news."

In sum, to succeed as a freelance professional, you must have the minimum required experience, skills, talent, and background required for the task. In most cases, this means either a bachelor's or similar degree and several years of working experience in the field or a related endeavor. Only in very specialized or licensed fields do you absolutely need advanced degrees.

≪ 4 ≫

HOW DO YOU GO OUT
ON YOUR OWN?

Most freelancers start part-time for many of the reasons or combinations of reasons discussed previously. Many also start haphazardly and, with hindsight and often chagrin, they find that they have wasted time, effort, and, most importantly, money that they could have saved if they had taken some simple steps and precautions.

≪ A HOBBY OR A BUSINESS? ≫

First, for very important tax reasons, you need to know whether or not your work should be considered a business or a hobby. As you can explore in more detail in Chapter 6, the Internal Revenue Service (IRS) does not allow the full range of business expenses and related deductions for hobby pursuits or investors that it allows for freelance businesses. You must have a clear business purpose in order to be entitled to all legitimate expense deductions. Yet, you must show the IRS that you intend to operate a profitable business that will, sooner or later, pay taxes on its net income.

To satisfy the IRS, you must show your intent to make a profit. Why? Losses from a hobby, such as collecting stamps or gold coins, are not deductible, although income from that hobby is taxable. For a legitimate freelance business, you can deduct expenses and losses that result in a breakeven situation. Consider this example: Suppose you are invited to speak at several conferences each year and you receive $500 a year in honoraria. Perhaps you make nothing. But your travel costs, including air fares, lodging, meals, taxis, and so on, totaled $2,000. Yet, your employer would *not* reimburse your expenses, pay you for the time you spent at the conferences, or consider your attendance at the conferences as part of your normal duties. The IRS could make a case that your speechmaking was a hobby. In that case, you could deduct only $500 in travel expenses; you would have to absorb the $1,500 loss. You could soon lose your desire to make speeches.

However, if you had established that you considered speaking engagements a separate business, you could take a $1,500 loss against your normal taxable income, saving you at least several hundred dollars in taxes under the 1986 Tax Reform Act rules.

≪ DEMONSTRATING BUSINESS INTENT ≫

You demonstrate that your activities constitute a business by intending to make a profit. This could be a Catch-22—how can you demonstrate that you want to make a profit before you do?—but the IRS has issued fairly clear guidelines. Years of practice have actually broadened the definition. Simply, you show intent by doing the things that a normal business does. When you are just getting started, if you do not incorporate, at least register a business name with your local government and take out a business permit or occupational license. Follow through by acting like a business: Establishing an office, in your home or office space; soliciting clients by sending out letters, making sales calls, buying advertisements, etc.;

and spending money on normal business operations. Even if you do not earn any income for the first three years, the IRS will still consider your activities a legitimate part-time business as long as you actively seek work and put forth sincere and provable effort.

Under tax reform, your business must show a profit in at least three out of every five years, but in many cases, if your income continues to increase and your business grows, but shows no profits, you can continue to qualify as a legitimate part-time business. Ask your tax advisor for the myriad details governing such situations.

The tax consequences are more fully discussed in Chapter 6, so suffice it to say here that you should definitely establish clear intent to do business and make a profit to protect yourself and your investment in any part-time freelance endeavor. The task is much easier with a full-time business.

≪ BEWARE OF THE EMPLOYEE TRAP ≫

The second most important thing you need to do is to make sure you are treated as an independent contractor and not an employee. The IRS can disallow many business expenses if it determines that you are actually an employee and not an independent or freelance contractor. It has strict guidelines that separate the two, and has been known to attack claims of independent contractor status. Follow the checklist given below to make sure you establish yourself as an independent contractor:

Freelance Status Checklist

▶ Does the client set your hours?
▶ Does the client determine where you must work, i.e., the location at which the job must be carried out?
▶ Does the client pay withholding taxes on your income?
▶ Does the client provide permanent or long-term working space that is not shared by other people?

- ▶ Does the client provide or pay for benefits, such as medical and health insurance, stock option plans, profit-sharing, etc.?
- ▶ Does the client refuse to sign a contract with you?
- ▶ Does the client provide a W-2 form at the end of the tax year?
- ▶ Did you fill out a W-4 form when you began doing work for the client?
- ▶ Does the client provide the equipment, supplies, tools, etc., that you need to get the job done?
- ▶ Did the client obtain your services through an employment agency, or through an employer services agency that provides its own employees to perform jobs for the company?
- ▶ Did you offer your services through a technical services agency through which Section 1706 of IRS code makes you an employee?
- ▶ Does the client provide a vehicle or other transportation for your exclusive use?

If you answered yes to *any* of the questions on the checklist, the IRS could question your status as a freelancer or independent contractor. If you filled out a W-4 form and received a W-2, you will certainly be considered an employee. If you answered yes to several of the questions, you greatly weaken your case.

Independent Contractor Guidelines

To avoid any doubts in the IRS's "mind," follow these guidelines:

- ▶ Always sign a contract that specifically states the job or project you will do, its deadline, and the amount you will be paid. The more specific the contract the better.
- ▶ Include in that contract a disclaimer that you are working as an independent contractor and should not be considered an employee.

▶ Make sure a client fills out IRS Form 1099-B when he reports the fees he has paid you. This form should be filled out between January 1 and January 31 each year for the income earned during the preceding calendar year.

▶ Make sure you have your own place of business, identified on business cards, stationery, and the like.

▶ Make sure you have registered a business name, even if it is just something like John A. Smith, Management Consultant, and have taken out an occupational license in your municipality or county.

▶ Make sure that even if you have only one major client, you solicit business from many others. The IRS will look askance at any freelance professional with only one client; it could claim you were deliberately avoiding paying withholding taxes, even operating with intent to defraud the government.

▶ In short, take all of the actions that an independent business would take.

≪ TO INC. OR NOT TO INC. ≫

One very definite way in which you demonstrate intent is the type of business structure through which you choose to work. Basically, you can choose from these legal structures:

▶ Sole proprietorship.
▶ Partnership (limited or general).
▶ Subchapter S corporation.
▶ Regular or "C" corporation.

Each has distinct advantages and disadvantages. You choose one over the other for two main reasons: (1) limiting personal liability and (2) tax benefits. You are almost entirely free to choose the best structure for you. This book provides some basic concepts and guidelines, but seek the advice of your attorney, accountant, and tax advisor before you choose. This book does not provide all of the details that affect your unique situation.

Sole Proprietorships

This structure is just like it sounds, a one-person business in which you are responsible for all debts and liabilities. But you are also entitled to all of the profits. You will have to register a trade name, pay for an occupational license or tax, get a sales tax certificate from the state tax department (if you have to charge your clients sales tax on the services you render), and, for many professions, obtain a state license.

Many freelancers believe a sole proprietorship is a bad idea because they remain liable for everything. That is true; everything you own, and not only the assets of the business, but cars, homes, property, equipment, etc., could be taken in a court judgment to pay off your business' unpaid debts or liabilities. Yet, in many cases, even incorporating to limit your liability against such suits may not help. For example, a writer cannot use a corporation to prevent being sued for libel, slander, or defamation. A writer remains personally responsible for what he or she states in print.

Even if you are incorporated, some clients may require you to sign a contract that makes you personally liable for your work anyway. You may be required to sign away your right to have a corporate structure protect you.

The best advantage of a sole proprietorship is that, unlike a regular corporation, you do not pay tax on your net earnings. Nor do you pay double taxation on corporate profits: once when they are made and again when they are distributed as dividends to shareholders; more than likely, you will be the only shareholder. You pay taxes only on the amount left after you deduct all legitimate business expenses from all sources of your income. You pay taxes only as an individual and at personal, not corporate, tax rates. Finally, you can take any losses in one business endeavor and subtract them from profits in another business.

For example, suppose that during your first year as a part-time freelance management consultant, you earn $5,000, but you spend $15,000. You have a net loss of $10,000. As a sole proprietor, you can apply that against your other income, say a $50,000 a year salary in your full-time job, and reduce your gross taxable income to $40,000.

You can also take full advantage of deductions such as office at home, equipment depreciation, automobile mileage, and many more that will be discussed in Chapter 6.

However, you do face limitations on deductions for health and life insurance for yourself and your family that a corporation can fully deduct. Yet, you would also qualify for a very favorable Keogh retirement plan or Individual Retirement Account (IRA), even if you qualified for and participated in a retirement plan at your full-time job.

Partnerships

If you plan to go into business with someone else, partnerships spread the risks of liability and the rewards of profits among more than one person. Partnerships do not pay taxes; the profits or losses are spread proportionally among the partners according to their shares or the terms of a partnership agreement. Partners then pay taxes at individual rates. However, under the tax reform law, your share of losses is limited to the *adjusted basis* of your partnership interest each year.

The adjusted basis for your interest is defined by taking your initial investment, adding your share of the firm's taxable income, increased liabilities and any additional capital contributions, and then subtracting any cash distributions or "draws" you receive, your share of losses, your share of the partnership's expenses, and your share of decreased liabilities. A partnership agreement can divide these shares almost anyway it wants as long as the potential losses do not exceed the legal limits. If you do not have a formal partnership agreement, the IRS will usually divide the profits and losses according to your initial interest or percentage of ownership.

Both sole proprietorships and partnerships, in which you have a 10 percent or greater interest, can set up Keogh plans, which have much higher contribution limits ($7,000 per year during 1987 and 1988) than an IRA plan. IRAs are limited to $2,000 a year or $2,250 for a worker and a nonworking spouse.

Partnerships have two serious problems:

▶ Liability for claims, damages, lawsuits, etc., are spread among the partners, unless a partnership agreement or a limited partnership arrangement limits each partner's responsibility. Worse, all partners may be liable for the actions taken by one partner, even if the others did not know of or approve of the actions.

▶ Personal problems with partners. Partners can get into serious disagreements—spouses divorce, business partners have affairs with the other partner's spouse, or simply, serious personal struggles break out. A partner can develop emotional or physical problems, and wreck the partnership. The only protection you have is a very detailed partnership agreement that spells out how such situations are handled.

Many people are firm believers in partnerships. They maintain that partners can complement the strengths and shore up the weaknesses of the other partners. For many years, the majority of law firms, accounting firms, group medical practices, architectural firms, professional associations (P.A.s), professional corporations (P.C.s), and the like, have succeeded. But the partners and members of these firms and practices, especially when they include more than two or three partners, should not be considered freelance professionals, especially when they include more than two or three partners. They turn into a different kind of organization beyond the purview of this book.

It appears from years of experience that the best small professional partnerships may be those in which the partners function independently. They have their own clients, they prospect for their own new business, they have their own assistants, they practice their own special skills which differ from those of the other partners, that is, they do everything that an independent professional would do. The partnership exists more so the partners can share office facilities and consult with each other than to bring the partners together as a close-knit team.

Each profession differs in its approach, and even small professional partnerships working as a team can succeed, but they can and often do face serious problems. It does seem that the best partnerships are established by people whose skills, knowledge, and personalities complement those of the other partners. Good partnerships tend to have an "inside man" and "outside man," that is, one is good at client and public relations, the other at administration, finances, and production.

Partners sharing the same strengths and weaknesses would simply overload a partnership. For example, suppose one partner in a three-partner group is very good at selling and public relations, and a second is reticent, but excellent at accounting and financial controls. Why would they need another partner with those skills and talents in the same firm? They wouldn't, although a third partner could help by bringing advanced knowledge or technological leadership skills in their field. Seek out partners who complement your strengths and shore up your weaknesses, if you truly believe you need partners.

Why go into a partnership in the first place? Perhaps the only real reason is when you find, by careful study, that your business will grow much faster than if you go it alone. This is not always the case; for example, freelance artists usually do better alone. You may simply not want to grow beyond your personal capacity to handle the work. You may not want partners because you are leaving the corporate world to avoid having to work with, answer to, or be responsible to or for others.

If you decide to enter a partnership, trouble can arise when partners fail to clearly understand their actual strengths and weaknesses. For example, suppose the partner whose true gift was for gab believed she was a technical wizard. It is highly likely that she would come into conflict—and use her verbal skills to win arguments with or browbeat—the real technical wizard.

Furthermore, as Chapters 2 and 3 indicated, true freelancers usually prefer to work alone. They tend to feel uncomfortable sharing both the responsibility and the glory with partners. They may prefer to suffer from their weaknesses and emphasize their own strengths rather than to go into partnership with someone else.

At least in the arts and editorial freelance fields, the author's experience and knowledge of others' experiences shows that the best partnerships are those with very close blood relatives or similarly enthusiastic spouses working together . . . and even they are not trouble-free.

If you work with a relative or spouse, you may find it hard to separate your interpersonal or family problems from your business situation. This is the single most significant difficulty of working in a partnership with a spouse or relative. Remember how Tom Smothers of TV and comedy fame accused his brother, Dickie: "Mom always loved you best." This has seemed very funny to millions of people for years, but the two work as partners in their act, and their act reflects the perils of bringing into a business months or years of unresolved personal and family problems. In fact, it was widely reported that the two Smothers brothers did suffer from jealousies and conflicts, causing them to split up for many years before they got back together in the mid-1980s.

Or take another example, if you have a fight with your spouse at 9 A.M., it is very unwise to bring that upset to a meeting with a client at 10 A.M. that you both must attend. A client may be able to sense the trouble between you and back away. Or if you are still mad at your spouse, you may actually do or say something to undercut his or her presentation.

Avoiding these conflicts most of the time requires a willingness to have a disagreement and either end it before you do business, or at least agree to delay it until you have finished conducting business for the day. Partners of any kind should never present a divided front to a client. Work out your disagreements within the partnership or family or agree to postpone the dispute before you make a presentation or meet with clients.

Despite these shortcomings, partnerships do offer many business and tax benefits that may mean more than any potential difficulties between partners.

Subchapter S Corporations

Subchapter S corporations are legal entities that limit the personal liability of shareholders while they pass through corporate income to shareholders as personal income. Usually this is very beneficial because your personal income tax rate is often lower than the corporate tax rate, and your liability is limited to your actual investment in the corporation. For most situations, plaintiffs (people suing the corporation) find it very difficult to break through a corporation and assault your personal assets. A corporation, as a legal "person," is responsible for its own debts and liabilities.

There are private and public corporations, too, but it is unlikely that a freelancer would sell stock to the public. You would incorporate as a closely held or closed corporation and own all or almost all (you may want your spouse, children, or family to own portions for tax reasons) of the stock in the corporation. S corporations are useful to transfer stock or equity to your family for estate and tax planning purposes.

Regular or "C" Corporations

The essential difference between a C and an S corporation is that your income from a regular C entity is taxed as a salary. You must make withholding tax payments and file W-4 and W-2 forms. Any dividends that the corporation pays will be taxed at regular income tax rates, and you must follow strict IRS rules governing salary sizes, dividends, and corporate reserves. Many owners have gotten into trouble with the IRS for paying themselves small salaries and large dividends (sometimes taxed at lower rates than earned income). Others have made the mistake of paying themselves small salaries and no dividends and holding back high profits as corporate reserves instead of distributing them as salaries or dividends to shareholders.

The burden of the C corporation is this: If you are the sole stockholder, you pay taxes three ways:

▶ Regular withholding taxes on your salary or earned income.

▶ Double taxation on your dividends because you pay both corporate taxes on net earnings before dividends *and* income tax on the dividends.

▶ Corporate income taxes on any net profits *before* the distribution of dividends.

Most freelance professionals choose S corporations to avoid this triple whammy.

The paperwork burden of the many additional forms that these requirements for a C corporation create often make it unattractive to freelancers as well.

Benefits of a Corporation

But either the S or C structure offers many benefits, including:

▶ You risk only what you invest in the corporation, not your personal assets.

▶ A corporation can stay in business after you die without any inheritance difficulties.

▶ It may be able to establish a better relationship with banks and have more borrowing power. At first, the bank will probably require a personal guarantee and collateral, but over time, a successful corporation establishes its own credit.

▸ Depending on your circumstances, corporate tax rates may be lower than an individual's. Consult your accountant or tax advisor to determine which type of corporation would best reduce your tax liability.

▸ Salaries and benefits paid to a corporate officer, who might otherwise be a sole proprietor, may be deductible.

▸ You can take advantage of a wider range of benefits, including pension plans, stock purchase plans, profit-sharing plans, medical and health insurance, life insurance, and other fringe benefits that a sole proprietor cannot deduct. Restrictions exist on some of these deductions for S corporations.

▸ You do not have to pay taxes on corporate income if no dividends are paid, eliminating the double taxation problem.

▸ If the business fails, you can deduct stock losses from your income tax.

▸ You may be able to shelter a large portion of your income in a pension plan.

Disadvantages of a Corporation

Disadvantages of corporations include:

▸ They can be relatively expensive to set up, $250 to $2,000 in legal fees alone, depending on the state and your attorney.

▸ Corporate income can be taxed twice, first as corporate profits and second as salaries you pay yourself.

▸ If a regular corporation loses money, you cannot deduct the losses from your income. You can do so with an S corporation.

▸ There are limits to how much protection a corporation can offer. As noted, it will not protect you from libel, slander, and similar suits, or any suits related to contracts or agreements that you personally guarantee.

▶ Corporations must pay social security taxes and unemployment insurance on salaries they pay their employees. You must
deduct payroll taxes from any salary you pay yourself,
whereas partners and sole proprietors do not pay withholding
taxes. Instead, they file quarterly tax returns.

Clearly, of the available structures, the S corporation or a sole
proprietorship has the most appeal to freelancers. And an S corporation is the best of the two if there is the slightest chance that your
clients will sue you for nonperformance or any reason other than a
clearly personal problem like libel or slander. It would pay to resist
a client's demand that you agree to take personal responsibility for
any contracts.

As noted before, these structures are more complicated than this
brief discussion can describe, so consult with your advisors to discuss them in depth.

≪ ESTIMATING START-UP COSTS ≫

Once you have decided on a formal legal structure, you need to
consider how much money it will cost to start your freelance business. They can be divided into six categories:

1. Equipment and supplies.
2. Office furnishings.
3. Licenses and fees.
4. Insurances.
5. Deposits.
6. Miscellaneous expenses.

The following worksheet gives an example of how much you can
expect to pay for various expenses in each category. The worksheet
also gives you a space with which to develop your own estimate of
start-up costs.

Freelance Start-Up Cost Worksheet

This worksheet assumes that you will begin by yourself and work from your home. The figures in the example are based on rough averages determined from the experiences of the author and freelancers whom the author has interviewed, as well as average national figures on costs of office supplies, rents, insurances coverages, licenses, and the like.

Category/Expense	Sample Estimate	Your Estimate
Basic Equipment		
Profession-required[1]	$1,000	$_____
Supplies	500	_____
Office Furnishings		
Furniture[2]	1,000	_____
Supplies[3]	500	_____
Machines[4]	500	_____
License and Fees		
Occupational license	100	_____
Business permit	10	_____
Legal fees[5]	500	_____
Accounting fees	250	_____
Insurance		
Business contents[6]	100	_____
Umbrella insurance	70	_____
Deposits		
Business telephone[7]	300	_____
Utilities	50	_____
Miscellaneous	500	_____
TOTAL	$5,380	$_____

Notes:

[1]Artists' materials, engineers' blueprints, etc.

[2]Desk, chair, bookshelf, filing cabinet, typewriter/computer/printer stand, etc.

[3]Business cards, stationery, copier paper, pens, paperclips.

[4]Purchase prices of an electronic typewriter and calculator plus rental cost of a copier. Can reduce this by renting all of them, or using any machines you already own.

[5]For incorporation, drafting a sample independent contractor agreement, reviewing your plans. Don't try to do this without an attorney. You wouldn't do personal brain surgery, so don't try to be your own "Legal Expert."

[6]You need to separately insure all of the equipment and furniture, supplies, etc. used in the business. If you have a fire or flood in your home, and the insurance company finds out that part of it was used for business, it may not pay for that loss under a regular homeowner's or tenant's insurance policy. This amount is only for a deposit; this insurance usually costs about $250 to $450 for $30,000 worth of coverage, more if you insure for full replacement value.

[7]A low estimate for how much a local telephone company will require as a deposit and installation charges to bring one line into your house for business purposes. Even if you incorporate, you may be able to use your home phone for your freelance business as long as you avoid advertising in Yellow Pages or local media. If you rent office space, of course, you will have to pay business phone installation charges and deposits.

≪ START-UP ANALYSIS ≫

This total is a reasonable estimate based on many people's experiences. Your actual costs will vary according to your profession, need for special equipment and supplies, and personal desire or business need for office space. You should add at least $2,000 to $3,000 for office rental expenses and miscellaneous costs, if you decide to rent office space. Another point often not considered is the cost of a personal computer or similar microcomputer. Many freelancers already own one and just use that one in the business.

You should note several points about these estimates:

1. These are cash payments, not in-kind contributions of equipment, machines, supplies, etc.
2. The value of any equipment you bring to the business is added to the company's capital base and can be depreciated against your income. Depreciation is an accounting and legal concept that reduces the value of real property, such as office equipment, real estate, automobiles, etc., each year according to a formula that sets a value for used real property. The IRS and tax law sets the schedules or annual percentage rates by which you can depreciate any kind of property. For example, if you spend $5,000 for a microcomputer system, you may depreciate it over three or five years, and deduct from your gross income either $1,666.66 or $1,000 per year, respectively. This helps reduce your tax liability as you get started.

   However, one good feature of the tax law concerning equipment is this: If you buy equipment, you can deduct up to $10,000 of its cost in the year that you buy the equipment. If it costs more than $10,000, you can deduct $10,000 and depreciate the difference. Or, if it is better for your tax situation, you can depreciate the entire amount. Usually, equipment is depreciated on a straight-line three-, five-, or seven-year schedule, depending on the type of equipment. For example, if you buy office equipment worth $15,000, you can deduct as an expense the first $10,000. Then, you depreciate the remaining $5,000, say for five years, on a "straight-line" basis. That is, you can deduct $1,000 in depreciation per year for five years.

3. If you have good personal credit and you have been a manager for a well-known corporation, you may use your reputation to obtain trade credit for many of your upfront expenses for supplies. Trade credit is granted when a supplier of business products, such as office supplies, agrees to give you supplies without payment. The vendor grants credit to the "trade," that is, buyers like you. Trade credit is usually granted for 30 days, and some will bill you, adding 1 to 1.5 percent per month interest or service charges. Use this trade credit if you need it, but avoid any trade credit with severe payment penalties, such as 5 percent per month service charges, or 5 percent late charges.

4. If you must drive often to meet clients, you should anticipate higher automobile costs, such as gas and maintenance costs. If you already commute every day, you may save money if you do not have to visit clients each day and most of them are relatively close to your office. But one of the joys of freelancing is that every mile you drive for business—to and from clients, office supply stores, copy shops, printers, business lunches, etc.—is deductible from your gross income at 22 cents per mile. You will need to follow the strict IRS rules on business travel, but this can save you many hundreds of dollars per year. In short, the IRS rules require you to keep a diary of whom you visit, how many miles you drive each day, and how much regular maintenance expenses, such as an oil change, cost.

≪ SET ASIDE WORKING CAPITAL ≫

According to the Small Business Administration and academic experts, most businesses that fail do so because they are "undercapitalized," a six-syllable word for not having enough money in the bank when they started up. Before you begin freelancing full-time, it is very strongly recommended that you have in the bank or as liquid assets, such as stocks and bonds or other cash assets, at least three months' family living expenses and three months' business expenses. You can substitute a working spouse's salary for a portion of these expenses, but you should have an adequate nest egg. This prevents you from being forced to scramble desperately for business during the first few weeks you are in business. Of course, do not use that financial cushion to do nothing. Some people may need a dose of insecurity to spur them to action, but for most, it appears that financial insecurity just makes a difficult situation that much more difficult. They may spend their time worrying about paying the bills instead of generating and serving clients.

≪ START-UP PROCEDURE ≫

After you know what kind of legal structure will be best and how much getting started should cost, you can plan how to "open your doors" for business.

No-Compete Clause?

First, if you plan to start part-time, discuss your intentions with your employer. Determine the company's policies about freelance work. You may not have noticed it, but if you have an employment contract, you may have signed a no-compete clause that prevents you from working freelance or in the same line of business for a year or two after you leave the company. Or the company may have a policy that prohibits its professional staff from freelancing within the same industry or for any direct or indirect competitors. Even if your company has such a policy, it may neither be written down nor, as importantly, enforced. A company which has a policy, but allows many exceptions, may render its policy meaningless. In such a case, if it tried to enforce the watered-down policy against you, you would have a good legal case for discrimination and could win damages against your employer. Consult with expert legal counsel before you take such a step.

Available Freelance Work?

At the same time, ask whether or not your employer—perhaps through another branch, department, or division—has freelance work available. In freelancing, as in selling, your first customer is your best customer. So, if your relationship with your employer is good, the company could easily become your first freelance client, even on a part-time basis.

Second, do basic market research to find out whether a real market for your freelance services and expertise exists. A freelance scuba diver may have trouble finding enough work in Des Moines, Iowa, but a farm management consultant may have no trouble at all. Many freelancers find that they have to sell their services on a regional or national basis to make a decent profit. If so, be prepared for the increased expenses of national selling: proposals, postage, and overnight delivery charges; time delays while waiting for replies; potentially high long distance telephone charges; high travel costs; and the like.

The long distance telephone bill is this author's single greatest annual business expense.

Interview for Market Research

Interview potential clients and ask questions, such as:

▶ What kind of freelance or consulting work in my field do you now hire?

▶ What qualifications and experience do you expect?

▶ How often do you hire freelancers or consultants?

▶ Do you have plans to increase or decrease your reliance on independent contractors?

▶ Would you seriously consider proposals to increase that reliance?

▶ How much (hourly rate, per-job rate) do you pay consultants or freelancers?

If you cannot find enough potential clients in your area or region, use industry or association directories, or your own sources, to research the national marketplace. Then, consider whether the amount that national clients are willing to pay makes it worthwhile for you to travel that far. Freelancers who can bill at $100 an hour and get reimbursed for travel expenses can certainly afford to approach clients on a national basis.

The added bonus of your market research is that you will also identify "hot" prospects, and perhaps, be offered your first freelance assignments.

Study Information Resources

At the same time, study the available information resources, contact associations, and prepare (have designed, written, and printed) your brochures and selling materials. (*Note:* Some freelancers object to the use of the word "selling." They protest that they don't sell, but rather "offer services." The author contends, after some 12 years as a successful freelancer, that what you do is *sell* yourself and your services, often with a lot more vigor and more sophisticated sales techniques than a person who sells cars or widgets.) See Part II of this book to find extensive lists of business, professional and trade associations, reference works, and sources of information and assistance for all of the categories of freelance professions described here.

Set Up Legal Structure

Next, when your legal right to freelance is squared away with your employer, or if the employer puts up no objections, set up your legal structure, most likely a sole proprietorship or a Subchapter S corporation, and organize your office.

Write a Concise Mission Statement

Next, plan your approach. Base that approach on a concise mission statement. It should be very simple and direct, such as "My mission is to provide employee benefit consulting services to Fortune 2000 companies." Another example is the author's mission statement: "My mission is to provide information services to book and magazine publishers, advertising and public relations firms, and in-house and corporate communications and marketing departments."

Focus on Initial Markets

With your mission statement written out, you will be able to focus on your initial markets. Many freelancers try to spread themselves too thin at first, flying off in all directions. Instead, concentrate on what you have identified as the markets most likely to offer immediate prospects for profitable work. Once you establish a base, you can expand your services. I wrote magazine articles for two years before I obtained the services of a literary agent and sold my first book. It was another year before I began doing market research.

Plan a Reasonable Budget

Next, plan a reasonable budget estimate. Estimate both potential or probable income and expenses. Listed next are more than two dozen categories of potential expenses you face when you work freelance. Supplement this list to fit your special circumstances.

MONTHLY FREELANCE BUSINESS BUDGET

Potential Funds / Sources

Client fees	$ _____
Interest income	_____
Working capital	_____
Stock & bond sales	_____
Bank loans	_____
Credit card cash advance	_____
Other sources	_____

TOTAL　　　　　$ _____

Potential Expenses

Assistant's salary	$ _____
Bookkeeping fees	_____
Charge card bills	_____
Credit card bills	_____
Cleaning service	_____
Computer service	_____
Contract labor	_____
Entertainment, business	_____
Equipment purchases	_____
Fees, legal & acctg.	_____
Insurance:	_____
Auto	_____
Office contents	_____
Medical/health	_____
Disability	_____
Loan payments	_____

MONTHLY FREELANCE BUSINESS BUDGET *(Continued)*

Maintenance contracts   _____

Miscellaneous   _____

Office equipment   _____

Office rents   _____

Office supplies   _____

Petty cash   _____

Postage/shipping   _____

Subscriptions   _____

Taxes, quarterly   _____

Telephone   _____

Travel, business   _____

Tuition, seminars   _____

Utility bills   _____

TOTAL $ _____

≪ POUND THE PAVEMENTS ≫

With your plan in hand, start calling on customers. You may prepare your path with phone calls, letters of introduction, résumés or vita sheets, simple or sophisticated brochures, lists of references respected in the industry, and so forth. But you will still have to meet the potential client and sell yourself and your service. With this preparation, you can feel confident you will be able to get off to a fast and successful start.

≪ 5 ≫

THE BUSINESS OF FREELANCING

As a freelance professional, you face a very difficult task: You must try to be practically all things to all people. If you worked as a corporate manager, you had minions to do at least some of your bidding. You had assistants and clerks and personnel in other departments to do things for you. If you worked for a large corporation, you had a specific set of responsibilities, other people had theirs, and none of you had complete responsibility for every aspect of a project. Now you do. This burden may be the hidden reason so many freelancers cannot cope with their "freedom" and go back to work for corporations.

≪ CONCENTRATE ON FOUR ACTIVITIES ≫

Mastering the business of freelancing and successfully juggling myriad responsibilities is not only possible, but relatively straightforward. The secret is *Keep It Simple*. Boil down all of your tasks to their lowest common denominators and do only that which is most important. In freelancing, this means concentrating on four activities. All others should directly support those four, or they are extraneous and should be discarded. The four are:

▶ Getting new clients.
▶ Serving current clients well.
▶ Getting paid for services rendered.
▶ Paying the bills and showing a profit.

Any activity during business hours that does not contribute to one of those four should be ended. Suppose you are a freelance economist and live in Florida, but all of your clients are New York City financial institutions. It might be foolish to join your local chamber of commerce; you could not meet your clients there, nor gain goodwill for your business. Yet, it would consume "profit" hours. On the other hand, it might be very wise to attend the monthly meetings of a New York group of securities analysts—even if getting there and back takes a whole day.

Find the Right Niche

Part of your preparation process for going freelance was identifying your strengths and interests and weaknesses. Use the first two to find your market niche. Do *not* work on your weaknesses. Do not be tempted to believe that your business can survive, much less prosper, if you base your work on weaknesses that you want to turn into strengths. In short, work from strength—yours.

In retail selling, every smart merchant knows that you put your best-selling merchandise in front of the store, and your worst selling goods near, but behind, the bestsellers. They use the bestsellers to drag sales for the worst along. Do the same with your strengths and weaknesses.

Perhaps your forte is research and statistical analysis, but you hate to use the telephone. It would be foolish to base your freelance work on activities that require personal or telephone interviews. Rather, you would do best to provide work based on research of primary and secondary sources of information in libraries or available through data base networks. Or, with available financial resources, you can hire someone whose strengths complement your weaknesses. Alternatively, you could find a partner whose strengths in personal selling complement your strengths in research.

Hire the Right Person

Finding the right assistant to work part-time, yet carry a lot of the burden, will not be easy. You could find an experienced administrative assistant whose personal life requires part-time work; he or she could work four or five hours a day, perhaps. But avoid the temptation to hire someone too young and inexperienced just because they will accept a lower rate of pay. Remember that you are hiring an assistant to back you up; you do not have the time to teach someone the basics of an assistant's job.

On the other hand, don't overpay or treat your assistant too leniently just because you work at home and you feel generous. Experience shows that employees tend to take for granted what is given to them. A generous salary at the beginning becomes, in a person's mind, a matter of right. He or she will still expect pay increases even though they are already being paid top dollar for the job. So, start them somewhat lower and raise their pay gradually as their performance and your financial situation improve.

The author has worked both ways. With one assistant with excellent skills, I made the mistake of paying too much at first and acted very leniently, excusing lateness and poor quality work, even unexplained absences. But after she and her husband demanded a 33 percent pay increase, because they thought I was rich, I put my foot down. With the second person, I started out at a reasonable, but not excessive rate. I expected on-time arrivals and did not go out of my way to act leniently. This person did not come to the job with excellent skills, but she worked hard, learned quickly, and contributed to a significant growth in my business. I could get my work done because I knew when she would be at work and what she would be doing. In fact, in a few months, I could leave the office for an entire day to make sales calls, and she could handle all administrative matters. Yet, I never really backed off my expectations of her work, and her raises were not out of line with the local market. Yet, she was very happy to learn new skills and receive a fair wage, and I was happy to add to my client list and increase my income far beyond the wages I paid her.

Look for someone with the guts to tell you when something is wrong. And have the guts to not only accept the advice or criticism, but encourage it. Of course, make sure a person supports an argument or criticism with facts, *and,* more importantly, with suggestions on how to improve the situation.

And have some fun. One of the pleasures of working for a freelance professional appears to be the prestige of being the righthand "person" for an industry leader. Working in a pleasant environment and on many interesting and, you hope, challenging projects provides a far superior working experience to that found in the average office secretarial pool. Do not underestimate the intellectual stimulation working for you can provide for your assistant; use it both to weed out those who are not looking for challenge, and to entice those who are.

≪ USE OUTSIDERS TO ADVANTAGE ≫

When you and your assistant cannot handle some tasks, bring in outsiders who can. Hire outsiders to help you just as you want your clients to hire you as the outside expert who can come in and make recommendations or solve a problem.

Don't ignore your suppliers and vendors as sources of help. Perhaps an office supply distributor can advise you on how to set up your filing system and recordkeeping system. Perhaps the telephone company can help you learn better telephone sales and interview techniques. Virtually anyone from whom you are buying services and goods will be eager to tell you how to use them to best effect; usually, they will help you for free.

Consider asking local chapters of national associations with a direct impact on your work for help. Of course, you have to be careful not to give your clients away to competing freelancers or consultants. But you can often get good, neutral advice on where to find inexpensive office space, good prices on furniture and equipment, industry information, and the like. You may even find new clients from among people in related industries who attend the chapter meetings. Bankers, corporate advertising managers, and corporate marketing personnel—not only members of advertising firms—often attend meetings of local advertising associations. The same holds true for marketing, bar, accounting, and publishing organizations, among others.

Consider joining business and trade associations. As Part II shows, there are many more associations than you can possibly join and productively participate in during a lifetime. So, you have to "qualify" the associations and determine which offers you the best contacts with potential clients, the best sources of information, the best seminars and conferences, and the best reference materials and research library. Some associations offer group insurance coverage, credit-reporting services, discount buying programs, training courses and seminars, advanced study certifications, and the like. The largest associations in your field may assemble and disseminate specialized marketing or technical knowledge and publish well-informed newsletters, journals, or magazines. Any group you join should include plenty of potential customers. Belonging to a trade group does not guarantee that they will become customers, but at least, shared membership can open doors that might otherwise remain closed.

Trade associations also provide a forum where you can meet other people who are doing what you do. You can swap information, discuss trends, get excess work referred to you, and so forth. But be very wary of giving away too much. I have always been reticent to discuss current projects with other freelance writers because early experiences showed me that some writers are less scrupulous than others. In short, I have seen my story ideas appear under other writers' names, and those writers happened to be ones that I had talked with at a writer's group meeting.

Last, but certainly not least, you need the services of a good lawyer and a good certified public accountant (CPA). The lawyer can draw up incorporation papers, draft a model contract for you to hand to clients, and protect you from costly lawsuits. You need to be on a first name basis with your lawyer, and be able to reach him or her by phone when the need arises. A lawyer that you trust can help warn you about possible legal risks of your activities and prevent you from taking possibly illegal actions. If he or she cannot handle every possible legal situation, the firm should be able to refer you to a competent specialist in that field of law.

Just as you need a lawyer, you also need a good accountant or CPA. A CPA can identify serious financial management problems before they get out of hand, or, if you call him or her in at the eleventh hour, help you work out of your problem as quickly and efficiently as possible. Make it clear that you want to know the CPA's opinion of your situation when he or she does your tax returns or balances your books.

CPAs may also serve other freelance professionals or firms in related fields, and can serve as an excellent source of information about business trends.

Ask your CPA the tough questions, and you will probably get straight-forward answers. But it is up to you to ask the right questions, such as:

▶ How can I make maximum use of available retirement plans?
▶ How can I reduce my taxes by putting family members on the payroll?
▶ How should I handle equipment depreciation, or should I lease the new equipment?
▶ What is your opinion of my cash flow projections, annual budgets, and projections for future growth?

▶ Are there any tax shelters directly related to my business methods or field that I can take advantage of?

In sum, use outsiders to support your weakness in or ignorance of the law, accounting practices, and similar fields. But, use them only as needed, not as "security blankets." In a business sense, you can often "take two aspirin" and call in the morning. Or maybe the problem will have worked itself out by then. In short, be judicious about running to the experts, and running up their bills. Making these judgments will get easier as you gain confidence in your own ability to run your business your way.

≪ CONTROL THE PAPERWORK FLOOD ≫

As a freelancer, your most important asset is your time. You must manage it wisely. The key time waster in any freelance business is paperwork. Keep paperwork to an absolute minimum except when it can be used to your advantage. For example, you should keep all receipts, cancelled checks, and records of any income or deductible contributions for as long as the law allows the IRS to take action against you. Usually, this is three years, but in many cases, the statute of limitations is five, seven, or even ten years. It is recommended that you keep your tax records for up to ten years.

You should also keep records, receipts, letters, and such for all *current* projects with clients, but clean out your files, except for any absolutely essential material, as soon as the project ends. Freelance writers, authors, and journalists should note that they may need to keep their material on hand for up to two years after the date of publication in case of a suit for libel or a dispute concerning facts. This rarely happens, but when it does being armed with notes and original information is essential.

Most freelancers, however, are not in this situation, and can get rid of excess paper as soon as a project ends. Research by many major corporations shows that 85 percent of all paperwork is never again needed or used, and most of the rest is used so occasionally that it would be cheaper to reconstruct the information rather than search for it in the files.

But paperwork can be used to advantage, so use good judgment concerning what to keep. One of these ways is in disputes with suppliers or clients. Suppose you bought defective equipment and the vendor refuses to either fix it, replace it, or take it back. You need to establish a paper trail of correspondence, notes from telephone conversations, receipts, repair orders, etc., to prove to the supplier that he is at fault. But these would be extraordinary situations, and as soon as the dispute is resolved, the files should be thrown out. Keep the receipts for tax purposes.

Conquering the Daily Paper Flow

Follow a strict paperwork handling procedure for each document that crosses your desk. Screen every document, and do the following:

1. Act on it immediately. Reply to it, put it in a bundle of similar documents for later "batch processing," call about it, put it away for filing, or throw it out. Don't let it sit on your desk.
2. Divide papers into four categories, based on their urgency: (1) Have to; (2) should; (3) maybe; and (4) toss out. Another way to divide up documents is: (1) Do now; (2) act soon; (3) consider long-term; and (4) read later.
3. Put similar documents together and handle them in bundles or batches. Don't write one check for one bill and then go to something else. Don't file one piece of paper and then write one letter, put it in an envelope, and seal and stamp it, and go to something else. You can see how much time this back-and-forth would waste. Rather, set aside blocks of time to handle different tasks: An hour in the morning and an hour in the afternoon for making or returning phone calls; an hour once or twice a week to respond to relatively unimportant

correspondence; an evening once a month to pay bills and so forth, according to your own needs.

If you hire an assistant, hire someone experienced in sorting through documents, filtering unimportant callers from important ones and so forth. Use an answering machine for the same purpose if you don't have an assistant.

4. Set up suspense and tickler files. Set up a file for each day or week of the month, and put documents, notes, correspondence, etc., in the file with the date you must or want to handle the situation. Then, check each day's or week's file each morning and take immediate action on the items in that file. Once you have taken action, throw out the document. Use colored tabs, folders, or ink colors to indicate each category's priority. Do not use more than four colors (red, green, blue, and yellow or orange are best) or you'll need a legend to your own filing system.

   Complement the tickler files with a wall or desk calendar that identifies appointments, deadlines, and important actions you must take. Usually, a 30-day calendar will do with room to the side to indicate future deadlines or key dates.

5. Make up project management forms that list all of the pertinent information about each project, important milestones to reach and when, names and phone numbers of key contacts at the client company and so forth. Use these forms in conjunction with the files you gather for each project. Use them to manage the work flow so you are always on top of each project. Use the *same form* from the proposal stage throughout the life of the project until you receive final payment.

6. Reply to correspondence with handwritten notes on the original, or write out your own letters. If you hire an assistant, it may cost you $5 to $15 for you to draft or dictate *one* letter, the assistant to type and correct the letter, and type the envelope, seal, stamp, and mail the envelope. Unless a letter pertains to your essential activities—getting clients and serving

them well—don't bother. If you type faster than you write by hand, do that or whatever saves you the most time.

In short, make sure you control the paperwork, and that any action taken on a document helps you serve clients or find new ones.

≪ Managing Your Desktop "Real Estate" ≫

You can better manage the flow of paperwork if you have a well-organized desk or work area. The notion of a "clean desk" being practically next to godliness does not hold water for self-employed freelancers. By the same token, a cluttered desk with stacks of papers even hiding the telephone should be anathema as well. You can help yourself work most efficiently if you properly organize your desk.

In the microcomputer business, the space on top of a desk is considered "real estate," and personal computer companies advise their salespeople to "capture as much of that real estate as possible" for PCs and electronic gizmos. They want to replace traditional business tools—pens, pads, calculators, telephones, etc.—with PCs and electronics. However, although many freelancers use PCs, you should not surrender your desktop to electronics. Rather you should organize your desk to best support your method of working.

Consider following the lead of kitchen designers who have long known that the most efficient kitchen is designed as a work triangle. At one point is the kitchen sink, at the second the stove and range, and at the third the refrigerator. In modern kitchens, dishwashers are put next to the sink for maximum efficiency, and countertops and cabinets are arranged between the points of the triangle. You can do the same thing to create a very efficient office space. At the head point, put your desk; at the second point, and usually to the right, put any frequently used office equipment, from calculators to PC to copiers, or whatever you use most often; and at the third point, put less-used equipment and reference materials, or perhaps a small set of bookshelves. Outside the triangle put infrequently used filing cabinets, bookshelves, storage, and the like.

Concerning the desk itself, office efficiency experts have proven that most people (right-handed people in any case) work most efficiently if they place their most important items in the top right-hand drawer. Then, put items in drawers in an across-and-down pattern so that the least important items are kept in the bottom left-hand drawer. You will gain the greatest time savings with this organizational pattern.

You'll need to organize your desktop so that the most important items are within easy reach. Right-handed people should keep their phones to their left so they can answer the phone, yet take notes with their writing hand—without dragging the phone cord cross the note pad. Keep a note pad immediately next to the phone. Next to that, keep your telephone number file. A good tip is to cross-reference important names and phone numbers by person's name, company name, and perhaps subject matter or address.

Keep adequate supplies of small items—paper clips, pens, staples, stamps, etc.—within easy reach in a desk drawer or on top of a large desk. Keep current files, or files you need to reach on a moment's notice, within easy reach, perhaps in a file drawer on the right-hand side of a desk, or a file cabinet located next to the desk. Make sure you do not have to get out of your chair to find an important file or phone number.

Keep important reference materials pertinent to your business within easy reach, perhaps on a bookshelf to the left side of your desk or on a bookshelf fastened above your desk. If your clients call you often for market data or want answers to commonly asked questions, keep this information within easy reach so you can quickly refresh your memory while you seem to answer the client's question without making him wait for an answer. Telephone books, industry directories, key client information, an encyclopedia, dictionary, and the like should be on this reference shelf.

Use *shallow* in and out trays. Do not use these trays to let items that should be thrown out stack up.

Some people recommend L-shaped or double-drawered desks, preferably large enough to accommodate all of these items and materials. You can decide for yourself, but make sure that above all, your desk, chair, and furniture are comfortable. You have to spend hours there, and you can sharply reduce your efficiency if you sit in a chair that gives you a backache, use a desk you have to strain to reach across, or work at a computer stand that you hunch over to read a screen.

These details of handling paperwork and desk organization may seem picky to many, but compare the time you spend working the other way. Organize your office haphazardly for a week and then organize it according to these guidelines and measure the time savings. The savings should be very noticeable.

≪ MANAGE YOURSELF WELL ≫

As you stem the paperwork flood, you need to manage yourself even better. First, you need to know how to set priorities and when to take action. It may seem obvious, but instead of tackling the most important actions and making the big decisions first, many freelancers procrastinate or get bogged down in the little, niggling details. To keep your priorities straight, make a daily list in priority order. Then start at the top of the list and work down. If you cannot complete the most important priority at that time, do what you can about it, and then go to the next item. Go back to the top priority at the end of the day before you waste time on the bottom of the list.

You can usually avoid the little things in any case; very often, they will take care of themselves. Sometimes, you can let others decide for you how important a matter is. For example, you get a message on your recorder from a person you do not know who has not indicated what he or she wishes to speak with you about. At this point, you have no reason to interrupt your more important activities to call that person back *until* the caller calls a second or third time, indicating that the call is indeed important to that person.

Indeed, on the second call, he or she may leave a message that indicates the nature of the call. This maneuver may seem rude to some people, but it can save you a lot of time. Of course, if you set aside telephone time each day, and you have time to return the call, do so simply so your callbacks do not get out of hand.

≪ USE DRIVE AND TRAVEL TIME TO ADVANTAGE ≫

Many freelancers squander many valuable hours by not using the time they spend in their cars or traveling. When you travel, take along a pile of unread, yet pertinent, information from your office. You might find information that can lead to a new client, or help serve a current client better if you concentrate on pertinent information—business correspondence or publications.

You can also use time on airplanes or in taxis to write short notes to clients and potential clients. A very successful freelance package designer and seminar leader carries a stack of small notes and clippings from trade journals, newspapers, or other news sources. These clippings identify someone he knows or wants to know, or something a past, current, or potential client's company has done. He jots down a note of congratulations, brings some information to a client's attention or makes an inquiry on each clipping. He then puts it into an envelope, addresses it and stamps it. He may do 25, 30, or even 50 of these during a plane flight. He drops them in a mailbox at the airport after he lands, and goes about his business. You can rest assured that everyone of any importance in his industry knows this man's name, and most of them think very highly of him. This is an ingeniously inexpensive, yet fantastically effective promotional technique. Yet, it is not false or artificial. The man is really interested in his clients' progress, and he wants to make sure they know about any developments that may affect their companies.

You can also draft proposals, do long-term planning, practice presentations or speeches, and the like on airplanes.

The virtues of laptop computers on airplanes, however, are debatable. They can be useful if you must do a spreadsheet or something similar before you reach your destination. But they can be noisy and obtrusive and interfere with other passengers' work. They can be more annoying than the electronic games with which poorly behaved children litter airplanes these days. And they add to your luggage, and possibly your fatigue. That won't help you get off to a running start at the other end. So ponder carefully before becoming a computerized commercial traveler.

Gizmos in the car, however, are another story—as long as they are voice-oriented. (Everyone's seen people reading or writing while driving, but it's a poor idea, to say the least.) In your car, you can dictate correspondence into a micro-sized cassette recorder. You can listen to audio tapes of books or magazines. You can use a recorder to think out loud. The importance of using a cellular car phone while driving would depend on your profession. If you spend most of your time driving from place to place, you can make a good case for one. If not, it can be an expensive affectation. The same argument can be made for and against radio pagers. The best pagers will give you the number of the person calling and a short message. It is a mistake to use a pager or beeper to return every call that comes in. A paging system that does not help you determine the importance of a call or the identity of the caller so you can decide when and whether to call back could be more a hindrance than a help.

Your Top Priorities

All of these procedures are designed to help you concentrate on your most important activities. Here are the kinds of activities you should consider your most important priorities on any given day:

1. Completing current projects on or before deadlines.
2. Making calls, presenting proposals, preparing proposals, or taking any action that will generate new business.
3. Keeping in touch with key and current customers regularly.

4. Staying abreast of your market, competitors, market trends, technological changes, new business opportunities not only by reading and studying, but also by working in the field. Don't allow yourself to be chained to a desk. Visit clients and potential clients, get a feel for changes or future trends.

5. Asking yourself what sources your next new market and your next new customers will come from. Consider how you may need to change your service or your approach. Consider the impact of "hot" topics and long-term terms on your services. Answer these questions:

   ▶ What should I be doing that I am not doing now?

   ▶ What should I stop doing that I am now doing?

   ▶ How can I make better use of my time and resources?

   ▶ Where and how should I focus my energies?

6. Managing your financial resources.

≪ MANAGING FINANCIAL RESOURCES ≫

Use your accountant to help you maximize the return you get from your financial resources. He or she can readily identify trouble before it becomes serious. You should have profit and loss statements; quarterly, perhaps monthly, operating statements; budget comparisons; and cash-flow forecasts so you will know what action you have to take to prevent a cash-flow crisis. Many freelancers have never heard of a cash-flow forecast, much less used one. Simply, it estimates your need for cash to pay your bills during the coming weeks or months. If you cannot readily identify where you are going to get the money to pay the bills you already know you have to pay *next* month or the month after, you could use an accountant's help.

The Name of the Game Is Cash Flow

Frankly, cash flow—getting paid quickly and in the right amounts—is crucial to a freelance professional's success. While you wait 30 days or more for a payment, your suppliers are breathing down your neck. They want to be paid on the spot, or within 10 days, not 30 or 45 days. This is why having adequate working capital is so vital to any freelance business. You should use your working capital as a revolving short-term loan fund that you give your business. You borrow from it to pay off current bills, but replenish it when your clients pay you.

Cash flow does not take a mathematical wizard to figure out. Your cash-flow requirements will be far different from those of a major corporation. They can be divided into these four categories:

▶ Funds to meet current obligations, such as loan payments, outstanding trade credit, aged bills, salaries, quarterly or occasional insurance payments, etc.
▶ Funds to meet government requirements, such as quarterly federal, state, and possibly, local income tax payments; monthly sales tax payments; payroll taxes and unemployment compensation; etc.
▶ Funds to serve clients' requirements, such as for business travel or any short-term expenditures for which you can bill the client.
▶ Funds you can use to generate new business.

A cash-flow forecast simply takes the total of these four categories and compares it to the available cash or cash that you anticipate you will receive during the next month or two. If you need cash or your clients often take 60 to 90 days or more to pay, you need to take serious action to speed up collections. Use your assistant, your accountant, or your spouse to act as your collection department to call the overdue accounts and prod them to pay as soon as possible.

In most freelance businesses, payment within 30 days is the common practice. Any client that pays within 15 days or less is a rare and precious jewel and should be cultivated.

The Credit and Collection Crunch

However, some clients will not pay within 30 days, and some may not want to pay you at all. What can you do about reluctant or very slow payers? You may know what credit card companies and other businesses can do to you: Send a series of requests for payment in increasingly threatening tones; threaten to cancel your credit; put your credit status on hold; report your action or lack of it to credit reporting agencies; refer the situation to a collection agency, which in turn sends you a series of demand letters; and ultimately refer the matter to an attorney for legal proceedings.

Unfortunately, and you will see why I say unfortunately below, freelance professionals rarely find it wise to use these means. I have noted before that my worse collection experiences required the intervention of a Congressman in one case, and an absolute refusal to leave an office without a check in the second. I have tried to use a collection agency in one situation, and the agency, a well-known national one, even sent out two letters and made a phone call. But the client simply replied that there was a dispute over my work, and the client did not consider the money to be properly owed. So, the collection agency reported this to me, and declined to pursue the matter.

In freelancing, if you decide to call in a collection agency, you must be aware that you have decided to end the relationship. In many cases, if you simply send a letter demanding your money, you may end the relationship, and certainly, if you send a threatening letter, you will end it.

Since most freelancers deliver services, a recalcitrant client can always come back at you with a claim that you did not perform the required service according to the client's standards, or any excuse to avoid paying you. Then, you can get into a spitting match and wrangle for months without ever seeing a dime.

There are other, more subtle and much more effective ways to collect money owed you. For example, you can put into any contract a statement that you will be paid within 30 days of delivery of the service. That is an outside limit; try to make it 10 or 15 days. Of course, if you can negotiate an upfront payment or deposit and bill the client each week for hours worked and/or expenses paid, etc., by all means do so.

The catch with a contract clause is that the client can ignore it, and there is not a lot you can do to force him to pay on time. If a contract states 30 days, and a client takes 60, or even 90, days to pay, there is little you can legally do to force him to pay, if he does not want to pay. One steady client of mine promises—in its own contract—to pay within 15 days of acceptance of an article. Yet, recently, it took me almost two months to get paid. Why? Because one editor decided that she did not consider the article "accepted" until it had been line-edited and was ready for production, instead of when she had received the article and decided to use it. To make matters worse, the firm moved across town, and even after the editor finally accepted the article, according to her definition, the accounting department took two more weeks to get organized and start writing checks. Even worse, after all this, the accounting department managed to get the amount wrong, and sent me only *half* of what I was actually owed.

What did I do in the meantime, besides yell and pull out my hair? I made long distance phone calls once or twice a week to the editor and to the accounting department. I disputed the editor's definition of acceptance, I asked—many times—both the editor and the accountants to speed up payment, and I mailed a duplicate of the original invoice. There was little I could do to speed up the payment process. The amount I was owed was too small for either a lawyer or a collection agency to bother. In addition, the work for the client had been lucrative in the past, and promised to be lucrative in the future, so I did not want to jeopardize a long series of future assignments with angry demands or outrage over one payment. Since I was 1,000 miles away, I could not go sit in the client's office—if I had been nearby, I would have, make no mistake.

When I finally received only half of the amount owed, I called the accounting department again. This time, since it was their error, I could afford to use an icy, but understanding tone in my voice. I have found that when someone else makes a mistake, I get the best results when I note the error, but act with some mild forgiveness, for example, "You made this mistake. You only sent half of the payment. I know it must just be an oversight. Would you please check into it and send me a check for the rest of the payment as soon as possible?" Usually, this correct, but understanding approach works very well.

Find Out How It Works and Who Works It

I have learned that the collection process that works best for freelance professionals follows a pattern. You simply need to know and follow the pattern to get paid most of what you are owed relatively on time. Expect to get stiffed once in a while, but with these techniques, you can reduce your losses to a bare minimum. (By the way, unpaid and uncollectable freelance fees are not deductible as casualty losses on your income tax return. You may be able to set aside a small portion of your income for bad debts, but the IRS may question even this small step if you are a freelance professional.) The worse situation I have faced was with a small publisher who accepted my article and printed it, but closed down the publication before he paid me. This publisher, too, was a thousand miles away. I wrote several letters. I even contacted the head of the company that had purchased the unscrupulous publisher's subscription lists. But since the buyer had not acquired the assets and liabilities of the previous company, only the mailing lists, he refused to honor the commitment. Again, the amount was too small and the distances too great for me to take more drastic action. So, I simply took the loss.

As an aside, the best excuse I have ever heard was this: the publisher could not pay me because his accountant had the company checkbook in his car and he was on his way to Florida. That had a certain "poetic" appeal, so much so that I told him that if he did not have a check for me on his desk the next afternoon at 4 P.M., I was going to file a complaint of criminal fraud with the police. I got the check. Of course, that ended the relationship, but as I've said before, who wants to do business with people like that? Simply don't. You do not have to work for them. Good clients outnumber the bad ones in every field. Unfortunately, you sometimes do not know beforehand who is honest and who is not. But, you do find out and quickly.

These and similar situations are galling, and can make anyone upset, even mad as hell. But you need not feel powerless. You can learn each client's accounts payables procedures and turn them to your advantage. Here's how:

1. Always send in an invoice to the person to whom you report directly. I have learned that even if an invoice is not necessary, send one anyway. In collections, too much paperwork is better than too little or none at all. It also serves as a gentle reminder to the person to take action to process a request for your payment.

2. Call that person a week later, and make sure that the quality of your work is acceptable, and ask whether he or she has started the payment process. This gentle prodding helps him or her remember to take care of the paperwork. It often happens, too, that the person will say, "Oh, I lost your invoice. Can you send me another one?" Or "I haven't received your invoice. It must have gotten lost in the mail." Then, after you hang up, you grimace and send a duplicate invoice. Use this call primarily to make sure the client is satisfied and pave the way for the next assignment.

3. If you do not receive payment within the client's usual payment period, call immediately, and ask the person whom you serve if a problem has come up. If not, ask him or her to call the accounting department and prod them to speed up payment. Also ask him or her to call you back with a status report.

4. Within a few days, if no payment has arrived, contact the accounting department directly. Here is where the real

subtleties begin. Ask for the person in accounts payable responsible for your account; your account may be listed under your own name or your company name, depending on what you put on the invoice.

5. Speak to that person directly. Find out his or her name and speak politely, even cordially. Explain that you have not received payment for some time, and would like to find out what the situation is. Remember the accounting clerks' names. Listen to them and enlist their aid. Ask them questions such as, "If you were in my situation, how would you handle it? What would you do to get this payment?" Usually, people are willing to help and explain their procedures.

More importantly, if the accounting clerks learn your name, and come to know you as a real person, they are more likely to help you. They may remember that you are a freelancer, not a corporation, and they may move your invoice to the top of their pile. If they are choosing among a number of invoices to pay, they may pay yours instead of someone else's simply because they recognize the name.

6. Then, probe to find out how the accounts payable process really works. For example, one of my clients writes checks twice a month, on the 15th and the 30th. If I submit an invoice before the 30th of the previous month, I get paid on the 15th; if I submit an invoice between the 15th and the 30th, it is paid on the 15th of the next month. So, if I have a deadline on the 25th, I try to get my work in before the 15th of the month, so my invoice will be paid on the 30th. That saves me three to four weeks of waiting, including time for the check to go through the regular, and usually very slow, mails.

Another client prefers to have an invoice number on each invoice. I don't send out enough invoices to bother with a numbered sequence. My accounting does not need to be that sophisticated, but after my payment was delayed several times, I started putting a fictitious number on invoices that I send to that client just to satisfy his accounts payables procedures.

Remember this rule: Do *not* try to change those procedures to suit you *unless* it is an emergency, or a series of mistakes has been made. For example, one large corporate client, whose accounting clerks say they never process checks by hand, actually has a procedure through which, in an emergency, a manager can issue a requisition for a handwritten check, and the accounts payable department will issue the check in 24 hours. Miraculous in a major Fortune 500 corporation, but true. I have only taken advantage of this procedure once, and only after my invoice was lost three times and payment delayed for three months. Learn the normal procedures and make them work to your advantage.

When to Take Drastic Steps

Frankly, calling in collection agencies and attorneys is a waste of time *unless* the amount involved equals thousands of dollars. I have asked different attorneys to become involved in situations on several occasions, and all have declined to take my case unless it involved a minimum of $5,000. One attorney would not consider it unless it involved $25,000. When attorney time bills out at $100 to $250 an hour, you can easily see how simply asking an attorney to write a couple of threatening letters could cost hundreds of dollars.

Collection agencies may be more beneficial. They tend to work on a contingency basis. That is, unless they collect, you do not have to pay them. Usually, they charge between 25 and 50 percent of the amount they collect for you. Collection agencies, however, usually simply send out computerized demand letters and make phone calls. You would need a court order in most cases to seize any of a debtor's property. The service you provide is not guaranteed by any property rights, unlike an auto dealer who can repossess a car if one does not make payments. So, if a client chooses to ignore a collection agency's demands, you would still have to sue.

Even if you win in court, you still have to collect what is owed you. By that time, what most often happens is one of several usually bad situations:

▶ The client offers a settlement for anywhere from 10 cents to
  50 cents on the dollar.

▶ The client drags his heels in paying the amount that you won in
  court, and you have to get another court order forcing him to
  pay, or allowing the sheriff to seize his property. All of this
  may take weeks or months.

▶ The client goes out of business and you are out of luck.

▶ The client plays hide and seek with the sheriff. That's right.
  After you win a lawsuit to collect a bad debt, and get a court
  order for the sheriff, you still have to take out summonses with
  the local sheriff and have him seize property or bank accounts,
  and auction the property to satisfy your debt. Who is going to
  go to such extremes for an average freelance payment? Not
  many. The cost in time, trouble, energy, and cash is simply too
  great.

Give Him a "Black Eye"

One tactic that may work against small companies is to give them a
proverbial "black eye." If they do not pay, report them to Dun &
Bradstreet, local and regional commercial credit reporting agencies, the Better Business Bureau where the client is located, and any
trade associations of which the company is a member. Of course, if
you as an individual do this against a major corporation, you can
expect it to have little effect.

You can also put the rumor mill to work for you as well. Spread
the word among other freelance professionals in your field that the
recalcitrant client is a bad payer. Try to make it difficult for the
client to obtain the freelance professional help it needs. A client
may threaten to sue you for slander, but if you can prove that he, in
fact, did not pay you for six months when he promised to pay in 15
days, it is very unlikely that the client would want to air his own
dirty laundry in court. Or you can take a more subtle approach and
hint at difficulties with a client, without saying why. You can always
say, "I wouldn't work for XYZ Co. again as long as I live." When

asked why, you reply, "I'd rather not say. It is too painful to discuss. But I would avoid XYZ if you know what is good for you."

In short, collection agencies and attorneys tend to be ineffective as collection tools for freelance professionals unless the sums of money involved are large and you have the odds of winning in your favor.

The Serious Boomerang

Remember, too, that a client can refuse to pay for many specious reasons, and drag his feet for months. These reasons may include:

▸ You delivered poor quality freelance work.
▸ You delivered the service late.
▸ The client has not completed the formal acceptance procedure.
▸ You have not finished the assignment according to specification; *ad infinitum.*

The serious difficulty is this: In most cases, your client can do you a lot more harm than you can do him. If you can start rumors about him, he can do the same for you, usually in spades. If you sue, or even simply make too many demands, the client can drop you and subtly blackball you in your industry in ways that you could never prove. If your industry is highly competitive, or economic times are difficult, other freelancers may be more than willing to put up with the client's slow payment habits just to have the work. I have learned that the persistent, yet subtle approach in which you get to know the people and procedures involved works best in the long run, maintains good relationships, and most important of all, gets you paid almost all of what you are owed.

≪ THE OTHER NAME OF THE GAME IS BUYING WISELY ≫

If *cash flow*—and *collecting what you are owed*—are the two names of the game, the third and equally important name is *buying wisely.* You can sharply reduce the drain on your cash flow if you buy wisely. You may be able to spend as much as half of your dollar more wisely than you think you can. The cardinal rule is the same for practically every purchase: Shop around, analyze the differences, and negotiate price and terms.

Here are some useful tips to follow that will help you become a better buyer:

▶ Buy from multiple vendors, and let each know it has competition. You will then get their best prices for the quantity you buy; you may be able to arrange better payment terms, or use credit cards; and you may get better delivery schedules and terms.

▶ Buy in adequate quantities that give you the best price discount. This averages out to about a three months' supply of office supplies. You tie up too much of your cash and capital in inventory if you buy a year's supply. A very successful entrepreneur taught the author the concept of "Buy it when you need it." He was willing to pay an extra few percent when he bought in smaller quantities in exchange for even greater savings on inventory carrying charges. In terms of lost use of cash, inflation, and loss of net present value, you lose at least 1 percent per month on the value of any inventory of office supplies. Other experts estimate that the annual cost of $100 worth of unused inventory is $22, a costly carrying charge for unused staples, paper clips and stationery.

▶ Buy from wholesalers to obtain discounts even when you buy in small quantities. You can order office supplies, printing, stationery, etc., through catalog houses and local warehouse outlets at prices far below those charged by the retail office supply dealer. The difference may seem small, but a savings of 50 cents to $1 per computer ribbon mounts up if you use 50 to 100 ribbons a year.

▶ Shop around and get *written* estimates from at least three printers when you buy stationery, brochures, business cards, etc. Look for quality and delivery as well as price.

▶ Use travel agents to make business travel arrangements. They cost you nothing, yet have the expertise to find the best flights, accommodations, and meals for your purposes at the best possible price. They also may know the best frequent flier plans, the best airport lounges and other tricks of the trade. If you use an agent for business, you can probably help yourself when you make vacation plans as well.

▶ Shop for the best long-distance telephone service. Analyze each long distance companies' plans for wide area telephone service (WATS) if you make hundreds of dollars worth of calls a month. Determine which gives the best quantity calling discounts and rebates, offers the best and most efficient service for giving credit, and offers the most personalized service for the small businessperson.

▶ When you shop for equipment, follow the three-year buy or rent rule. If the payback on the equipment is three years or less, buy it; if longer, rent or lease. You save money in the long run, and with rentals, you can easily and quickly upgrade to better equipment. With leases, you can also change to better equipment at the end of the lease.

▶ Buy for the task at hand, not the promise of future expansion. For example, it is foolish to buy a personal computer if you rarely write letters, never do spreadsheets, only send out bulk mailings once or twice a year, and so forth. An inexpensive electronic typewriter is more than adequate for your assistant's and your own requirements. Do not buy now in the expectation that a year from now you will have grown so rapidly that a computer, a high-speed copier, or any of many electronic gizmos will ease the burden on your huge staff.

▶ Lease equipment when you can with no security deposits, no personal guarantees, no separate third-party agreements, and no payment escalation clauses. If you buy, buy on installment terms or take a bank loan. With leases and loans, you let the business and your success pay for your equipment, and you do not waste your upfront capital.

▶ Avoid expensive, long-term service contracts with the equipment manufacturer, if plentiful and inexpensive alternatives are available. For example, it is foolish to buy a typewriter service contract for one typewriter when you do not expect it to break down except once every two or three years. Pay for repairs as they occur.

In short, keep your overhead down and run a lean office, having only the staff and equipment you need to succeed now.

≪ PROTECTING YOUR SUCCESS: INSURANCE COVERAGE ≫

Many freelance professionals trust their own skills and talents to guarantee their success. That is as it should be. But what happens to the business—and more importantly, your family—if something happens to you? In short, you need adequate, although not extravagant and expensive, insurance coverage to protect you, your business, and your family in case of emergency or unforeseen events. Following are the types of insurance you will almost definitely wish to have; the next section displays some options for later consideration:

Life Insurance

You should have a large (in excess of $100,000) term life insurance policy on your life if you are under the age of 40. Term life is the least expensive type of life insurance, and a large policy guarantees that your family can pay off your debts, close down or sell the business, and still live comfortably while they make the transition to a new lifestyle without you. As you get older, you should investigate universal life, whole life and other types of policies that build value as you pay for them. Term life does not build any cash value. During 1987, there was an upsurge in the purchase of single-premium life insurance policies as a tax-free investment. If you have the capital to spare, a single-premium policy can save you a lot of money in the long run, but they do violate the principle of pay-as-you-go to preserve capital.

Major Medical and Health Insurance

If your spouse continues to work, and can cover you under his or her policies, take advantage of them to reduce your costs. If not, buy the minimum amount of medical and health insurance that will cover any serious illnesses. If you have children, you will need more extensive and more expensive coverage. Anticipate that, under normal circumstances, major medical and health insurance will be one of your greatest costs of doing business.

Remember, too, that many trade, professional, and business associations offer relatively low cost health and major medical insurance coverages.

Fire and Comprehensive

As noted earlier, you need to insure the contents of your office for replacement value. Insurance companies usually enforce a "co-insurance" clause which limits your reimbursement to 80 percent of the depreciated value of the contents. Very few policies will pay for the cost of reconstructing documents and papers. You may lose a manuscript worth $10,000, but the insurance company will only pay you for the $15 worth of paper it was printed on or the $5 computer disk on which it was stored. Have an insurance broker study the policies carefully and match one as well as possible to your unique situation. Use policy "riders" to add coverage for esoteric equipment or objects, such as photographic equipment or art works. The coverage will be expensive and you will have to pay for an appraisal, but the coverage will be worth it in the event of loss.

Liability

You need many kinds of liability insurance, including personal, property, auto, and business. Even if your office is in your home, if an assistant should trip and fall, or a client should have a heart attack, you should expect to be sued for liability. We live in a litigation-happy age, and worse, judges and juries make outlandish awards. So be prepared to carry at least the legal minimums, or better, the limits recommended by your insurance agent.

Worker's Compensation

Even if you have only a part-time assistant, it is wise to pay for state-provided worker's compensation insurance to avoid disability and liability suits.

Automobile Insurance

If you use an automobile exclusively for business, and especially if you allow an employee to use it, you may need commercial vehicle insurance. If you are incorporated, you may want to register your car in the corporation's name and have its own insurance, although it will be more expensive. If you have an accident during the conduct of business, the corporation can protect you from personal liability. On the other hand, most personal auto insurers charge very little to add coverage for drivers who do not own the car or are not members of the owner's immediate family. Consult with your insurance broker to find the best coverage for the lowest price.

Umbrella Insurance

This type of insurance is a general-purpose liability policy that provides coverage over and above other policies. For example, suppose your auto liability policy had limits of $300,000 per person per injury. You have an accident in which a passenger is permanently disabled, and the victim sues you. The victim wins a judgment for $750,000. An umbrella policy basically would pick up the difference between the $300,000 limit of your policy and the total award.

Note that umbrella policies may require you to have relatively higher limits—more than the legal minimums—for your other policies. This reduces the umbrella insurer's risk, but raises the cost of the initial coverage. But any self-employed person should have a $1 million or greater umbrella policy to protect against all kinds of weird accidents and lawsuits. Fortunately, most umbrella policies are inexpensive, less than $100 per year for $1 million coverage.

Advisable, but Optional, Policies

You can tell that insuring yourself, your business, and your family as a freelance professional may be an expensive proposition. It may be the second or third largest, if not the single largest, item in your budget. Yet, you may need more coverage, especially if your spouse does not work and you have children. Consider these policies to give them added protection:

Key man insurance. This policy pays an amount large enough to help keep the business operating if you die or become permanently disabled. It usually provides enough money to hire a manager, arrange for the sale of assets and so forth. If your business does not readily transfer to another person or company, you may not need this type of insurance.

Business interruption. If your business is interrupted by a fire, natural disaster or, in some cases, your temporary disability, this kind of policy will pay your company's basic bills—rent, outstanding bills, telephone, utilities, etc., so you can keep the doors open until you recover or reestablish the office. Usually, this kind of insurance is purchased by manufacturing companies, and it can be relatively expensive if you buy a small policy.

Personal disability. This policy pays a sum toward your living expenses while you are disabled. If you are permanently disabled, you are eventually transferred to social security and federal disability insurance, but for the first six months to a year, you can cover part of your living expenses. However, the author has found it very difficult to obtain adequate disability insurance at a reasonable price. One insurer planned to charge $900 per year for disability payments equal to at most $900 per month. This is a very high rate. In another example, an insurance company refused to grant a request for $2,500 per month disability coverage, although records showed that the person's fixed monthly living expenses exceeded that amount. In short, you may need disability coverage if you have children and your spouse does not work, but, if you work as a freelance professional, expect it to be hard to find and very expensive. The easier alternative is to sock away in an inviolable bank account, as soon as possible, the equal of six month's living expenses, and insure yourself.

Business theft. If you have any employees and deal in any large amounts of cash or negotiable checks, you need business theft insurance to protect yourself from employee theft. A trusted assistant could forge your name on your business checking account and make off with your cash and reserves either little by little or in one big "hit." It is unwise to let just one employee handle your funds or go to your bank and cash checks for you. Do not allow an assistant to also act as bookkeeper, and never give an assistant the power to sign checks in your name or on their own.

≪ How to Control Insurance Costs ≫

Fortunately, you can control high insurance costs in many ways. Follow these tips to reduce your insurance costs so you can obtain the unusual coverages you really need:

1. Insure yourself as much as possible. Determine how much of your savings you can afford to spend on minor emergencies, especially things like doctor's bills, used car repairs, minor thefts, minor damages, and the like. You could set up an

interest-bearing account that sets funds aside for this purpose. Large companies more and more often are adopting
"self-insurance" programs which set up similar, but much
larger, pools of money to cover their risks.

2. Another way to self-insure is to have very high deductibles for
your important policies. For example, if you do not have any
children, or if your wife does not expect to become pregnant,
you can reduce your medical and health insurance premiums
by 60 to 80 percent per year with a high deductible. In
essence, you agree to pay the first $2,000, $5,000 or even
$10,000 of your hospital and medical bills. Most people, of
course, have very low deductibles of $100 to $250 because
they have children with frequent doctor's bills, or they cannot
afford to pay out large amounts of cash for hospital bills or
medical emergencies.

But if you can afford the cash outlays—against any type of
"accident"—you can sharply reduce your annual premiums.

3. Use an independent insurance broker or agent who can
search for the best policy at the lowest possible cost. Independent agents can often choose from among dozens of policies from a variety of companies. Therefore, their primary
interest is making you, and not an insurance company, happy.
There are, however, exceptions for certain kinds of policies in
certain parts of the country. For example, insurance on certain types of automobiles was so difficult to obtain in Florida
in 1986–1987 that one was well-advised to take anything one
could get.

In general, though, it is best to shop around with both independent agents and salespeople from major insurance companies to get the best deals. Then, every two years or so, review
your policies and invite other agents to make bids and proposals. The insurance market changes very rapidly these days,
and in many ways, rates are falling dramatically. You need to
have a broker stay on top of the situation for you, while you
retain the flexibility of finding a new broker if your current

one does not provide good service or is not able to deal with an adequate array of insurance carriers.

4. Look for loopholes. Many insurance policies are written with gaping loopholes. Consider, for instance, that most product liability policies do not cover accidents in foreign countries. Suppose you own a small mail-order operation, and the product harms a buyer in France. The injured person could bring suit in French courts, and your U.S. product liability policy would not cover you. You could go bankrupt paying foreign attorneys' fees much less any settlements or judgments. In short, find the gaps in coverage by reading the fine print and closing them as well as possible. Use your broker's experience to help do this.

5. Use worker's compensation to provide employee disability coverage. For one-person operations, this is the least expensive way to provide disability coverage for any employees and offers very good protection for you from more serious lawsuits.

6. Obtain replacement value policies where the additional cost is reasonable. As noted, most policies only pay 80 percent of full value minus depreciation. In other situations, an insurance company may force you to allow it to pay only for repairs to equipment, furniture and furnishings, not replacement or even 80 percent of the full value of the equipment or item. Insurance companies, if policies allow them, will reduce to a minimum what they have to pay and how soon they have to pay it. So, it is usually a good idea on auto and business contents policies, or "rider" policies for equipment, to obtain replacement value coverage. And also check into the company's standard time lag for paying claims.

7. Look into trade or business association group insurance policies. Very often, an association will obtain very favorable rates for common types of policies, or policies of particular interest to your industry.

8. If you have any employees, or you employ family members, consider group insurance policies for important policies. You can buy group policies for groups as small as two or three people. Consult your broker to see if you should take advantage of any opportunities for group insurance if you incorporate.

9. If your spouse works, take full advantage of any low-cost or free insurance policies that the company provides. Avoid overlapping coverages because the insurance companies will not pay twice for the same claim; accepting payments from both, under these circumstances, would be illegal and immoral.

    With the right combination of insurance policies, self-insured funds and high deductibles, you can arrange adequate protection for yourself, your business and your family when you start your career as a freelancer.

≪ EARLY SIGNS OF TROUBLE ≫

With these business techniques and organizational tips, you should launch your new freelance career smoothly and well. Yet, you can recognize early signs of trouble that you should take immediate action to solve or prevent. Use these signs as "early warning radar" to avoid getting in over your head before you have a chance to get your feet on the ground:

Checklist for Trouble

1. You are very confused about what to do next. Your desk is piled high with paperwork.
2. You have very little cash in the bank and no plan to obtain enough to create at least a month's cash reserves.
3. You simply feel unhappy or depressed. You have a very hard time making sales calls and you frequently miss deadlines.

4. Your expenses continue to climb while your income sinks or remains stable. You are paying business bills with your personal savings and/or your spouse's income.

5. Your clients often send back your work for revisions or are critical of its quality.

6. You have plenty of assignments or projects to complete, but none of them ever seem to get done.

7. You do not have a written plan to generate clients, or you have strayed far from your original plan without rewriting and thinking through your change in direction.

8. Most of your accounts receivable have stretched to 60 or 90 days, and your current bills or payables have begun to age past 30 days.

9. Your assistant reports late to work very often, does not do assigned work on time or accurately, and complains about working conditions.

10. Family members express hostility or unhappiness about your work and your progress or lack thereof.

All of these signal a serious problem that can at best undermine your ability to meet your obligations and at worst drive you out of business. Be willing to recognize these symptoms of a "diseased" business and take steps to cure them. Here's how:

▶ Develop a written business plan with which you will launch your business.

▶ Organize your work carefully each day.

▶ Think through the directions in which you want to go.

▶ Keep expenses down and sustain cash reserves.

▶ Adopt an attitude of belief in what you are doing and act enthusiastically even when you don't feel like it.

▶ Pay attention to details and the quality of your work even if you have to work long hours to meet deadlines.

▶ Follow clear work schedules and set milestones so that you complete projects on time.

▶ Aggressively collect the money owed you as soon as an invoice or bill ages 30 days.

▶ Give your assistant challenging tasks, or find a new assistant if his or her work and attitude does not improve.

▶ Set aside time to spend with your family, and act sensitively to their fears and concerns about their new insecurity.

If you are going through more than one or two of these situations, you could use your accountant's or business advisor's assistance to get back on the right track. It's tempting, as a freelance professional, to become a "jack of all trades." But a wiser course is to become a "jack of most trades," and training yourself when to look for help, and where to seek it. Only then can the tips and techniques in this chapter help you develop your own efficient and profitable business operations.

≪ 6 ≫

TAXING MATTERS

The 1986 Tax Reform Act destroyed some freelance tax shelters, and made others more difficult to take advantage of. But it did not harm, and in some ways enhanced, this essential principle: Your own business is still the best tax shelter available for the middle class. Regardless of the type of business structure you choose, freelancing makes available tax deductions that employees can't even dream about.

However, this chapter does not purport to give formal or specific tax or investment advice. The discussion of tax matters in this chapter is solely for the purpose of alerting freelance professionals to the opportunities and difficulties present in tax laws, rules, regulations, and court actions that may affect their businesses. For specific advice on these or any matters related to taxes, consult your accountant, CPA, attorney, or qualified tax advisor.

≪ BUSINESS EXPENSE DEDUCTIONS ≫

By and large, with the exception of the widely publicized business entertainment and travel rules, the 1986 tax reform law did not disrupt most commonly accepted business deductions. Here are the categories of business expenses given on Schedule C, *Profit or Loss from Business or Profession,* the IRS schedule for the self-employed sole proprietor. Partnerships and joint ventures must file Form 1065, but the deductions are very similar.

Items Generally Accepted as Deductible

Advertising

Bad debts from sales or services

Bank service charges

Car and truck expenses (See explanation of special rules later in this chapter.)

Commissions paid to independent sales representatives

Depreciation (from Form 4562 for equipment, vehicles, furniture, furnishings and improvements and subject to new, tougher rules)

Dues and publications (Employees have a more difficult time deducting these now, but not freelancers.)

Employee benefit programs

Freight, shipping, delivery and postage charges

Insurance for business. (New rules for personal medical insurance for sole proprietors discussed below.)

Interest (both mortgages on business real estate and installment loan payments)

Laundry and cleaning

Legal and professional services (For working people, the cost of tax return preparation is only partially deductible now; it is much more deductible for freelancers.)

Office expenses

Pension and profit-sharing plans

Rent on business property

Repairs

Supplies

Taxes

Travel and entertainment (subject to the tougher rules, but with significant loopholes for corporations)

Utilities and telephone

Wages and salaries

Other categories, such as:

▶ Contract labor (payments to a temporary employment agency or other independent contractors)

▶ Service contracts, which could be included under repairs

▶ Home office deductions, for which special rules apply

▶ Moving expenses (still fully deductible for you personally as well, but with limitations on how often you can do this. Always deductible for a business entity no matter how often it changes location.)

Of course, you can also deduct the cost of goods sold and/or the cost of your operations. These deductions include: materials and supplies; cost of labor; inventory purchases; and the like.

In general, every penny you spend to conduct your business is deductible, with the relatively well-known exceptions. Most of this chapter will concern these special exceptions and the detailed rules that the IRS applies to them under the new law and in enforcing regulations.

≪ NEW BUSINESS ENTERTAINMENT AND TRAVEL RULES ≫

Perhaps the biggest change for freelancers comes from the new travel and entertainment rules. This rule was the subject of intense debate, and the actual results make it somewhat more difficult, but not impossible, to deduct these expenses. And in one case, a loophole still exists for freelance professionals who have incorporated. Here's how the new rules work:

The law limits deductions for most business meals and entertainment to 80 percent of the total cost. The tough part is this: The expenditures qualify as business-related *only if* business is actually discussed during the meal or entertainment. Fortunately, the cost of business transportation, including everything from air fares to taxi cabs to auto mileage, remains 100 percent deductible. But travel to investment seminars or conventions does not qualify unless your profession or career is that of investment advisor, stockbroker, stock analyst, or similar endeavors. Private investors can no longer deduct these costs.

Here are some examples that will illustrate the 80/100 rule:

Expenses	Deductibility (%)
Lunch with client, business discussed before, during or after meal	80
No business discussed	0
Cab fare to restaurant	100
Train fare to nearby city	100
Auto mileage (22 cents/mile)	100
Air fare to Boston for consultation	100
Hotel in Boston	100
Meals in Boston by yourself	80
Meals with client, business discussed	80
Meals with client, no business	
Client's meal	0
Your meal	80
Suit damaged, new suit purchased	100
Cost of cleaning soiled suit	100
Air fare for attorney to attend legal convention	100
Meals, alone	80
Tickets to football game for *you* and client, business discussed	80
Transportation to game	100
Meals, drinks and food	80

Expenses	Deductibility (%)
Free tickets to ballet for client (You are not present)	0
Lunch for yourself at Rotary Club	80
Golf at country club with client, greens fees, carts, foods, beverages, portion of country club dues, business discussed	80
Tickets to charity ball run by volunteers	100

The Recordkeeping Kicker

The real kicker to the new business entertainment rules involves recordkeeping. These rules are much stricter than before for all business meals and entertainment costing more than $25. Under the old rules, you could prove meal expenses with a credit card, a canceled check or a restaurant check stub plus some other record such as a diary entry. If the meal had a general business purpose and took place in surroundings conducive to business, it was deductible. An actual business discussion did not need to take place. Now, you must provide specific information for *each* business meal or entertainment occasion. You must have a *substantial* business discussion before, during, or after the meal or the entertainment. In addition, you must show that the meal was associated with the *active* conduct of your profession or business. In this situation, you must show on receipts:

▶ Amount you spent—totals are fine.
▶ Time, date and place of meal or entertainment.
▶ Nature of the business discussion, the business reason or the nature of the business benefit. TRAP: Having lunch to keep a client's good will is no longer a sufficient reason to deduct a business meal.
▶ Identification of people who participated in the business discussion, not just the meal.

Here is a good example of the proper documentation: January 1, 1988, 12:30 P.M., lunch ($57.50), tip ($12), at Trendy Restaurant with President Jones of XYZ Inc. to complete discussions and negotiations for new contract which were begun in his office at 11 A.M.

However, and fortunately, business meals which cost less than $25 are *not* subject to the same rules. You still must have a record of who you dined with and the business purpose, but you do not need a receipt or a detailed discussion.

In any case, you should now keep a thorough diary which lists the details of all under-$25 business meals, and it is best to support a diary entry with a restaurant receipt that shows the amount, date, location, and name of the eatery.

In short, when in doubt, document with as much detail as possible.

TAX TIP: Thorough recordkeeping is more important than ever. In the past, you may have overlooked many small business meals and forgotten to deduct them. By keeping complete, strict and accurate records, you may save yourself business meal deductions you would have missed or ignored in the past.

TAX TIP: If you set up a corporation, you need to know how to avoid a tax trap. Under tax reform, a limitation applies to deduction of business expenses, including meals and entertainment. You can deduct only those business expenses which exceed 2 percent of your adjusted gross income (AGI). Thus, if your adjusted gross income from the salary your corporation pays you is $20,000, you cannot deduct the first $400 in personal business expenses. However, if your corporation provides an expense account and reimburses you as an executive of the corporation for your business meals and entertainment, the corporation can deduct 80 percent of the cost of meals and entertainment and 100 percent of the cost of travel, all according to the new rules. Yet, you do not have to pay taxes on the value of the reimbursed expenses.

NOTE: This reimbursement rule also applies to subscriptions, dues, local travel, and so forth, so you should set aside a more liberal expense account in your corporate budget. Do *NOT* pay for these items out of your own pocket unless you seek reimbursement from the corporation with a company check.

≪ IMPACT ON BUSINESS AND EDUCATIONAL TRAVEL ≫

As you can see from the example, business travel expenses are not as badly affected as meals and entertainment with the exception of general educational and investment seminars. Yet, there are some stricter rules concerning mixed business and vacation or leisure travel expenses.

First, if business is your primary purpose, you can deduct 100 percent of your local and long distance transportation and hotels or lodgings. If your spouse accompanies you, and is *not* an employee, a business partner, or part-owner, you cannot deduct his or her individual air fare, but you can deduct the entire cost of the lodgings and any *shared* car rental, taxicab or local transportation costs.

Second, if a vacation is your primary purpose, you cannot deduct anything, except the cost of occasional meals with clients. For example, suppose you and your spouse take a vacation to London, but visit and have lunch with the branch manager of one of your clients in the United States. You can only deduct 80 percent of the cost of the meal, *if* you discussed business during the meal. You can include tips, parking lot fees and taxes when you calculate the 80 percent amount. And the cost of local transportation to meet the branch manager would still be 100 percent deductible.

The key, of course, is how the IRS defines the words *primary purpose.* Use your common sense and tax advisor's judgment to decide which expenses really are deductible.

Your spouse can deduct the cost of his or her travel with you if:

1. You both own the business.
2. The spouse is fluent in the language of a foreign country in which you do business.
3. The spouse is employed by the business.

4. The spouse performs business services that cannot be otherwise obtained.

However, you cannot deduct a spouse's expenses if he or she simply answers the phone, types or runs errands.

Concerning educational travel, you can deduct them like business expenses if you work in a field, trade or business that is the subject of the seminar or training. You cannot deduct the cost of attending a general seminar, or an investment seminar. Teachers can no longer deduct foreign travel simply to enhance their general understanding of a country's culture and language, unless he or she is a foreign language teacher and takes specific courses in a school or college in that country.

Rules governing records for business meals and entertainment definitely apply to these expenses incurred while you travel.

≪ THE DEPRECIATION OF DEPRECIATION ≫

Before tax reform, freelance professionals could take advantage of very liberal investment tax credits and accelerated depreciation rules against the value of real property, equipment, vehicles, furniture, furnishings, etc. Tax reform did away with these advantages and substituted tougher straight-line depreciation rules on real property and equipment. It did bring one change of benefit to freelance professionals: you can now deduct as an expense the first $10,000 you spend each year on equipment, company cars (subject to other rules on the deductibility of luxury cars) and the like. For example, suppose you spent $7,500 on a new personal computer system. Under the old rules you could have taken a $750 tax credit (10 percent ITC), and depreciated the remaining $6,750 over five years. Or you could have deducted the first $5,000, taken a tax credit of $250 on the $2,500 difference, and depreciated the remaining $2,250. Today, you can deduct in the year you buy the equipment the entire $7,500, even if you actually borrow the money from the bank to pay it.

If you buy equipment worth more than $10,000, then you depreciate the difference, for example, on a $25,000 piece of equipment, you would depreciate $15,000 in five equal amounts, or $3,000 per year. *NOTE:* Your deduction for equipment costs cannot exceed your annual income to create a paper tax loss. If you earn a net income of only $8,000, and buy equipment worth $10,000, you can only deduct $8,000 in that year. You can carry forward the remaining $2,000 to apply against future years' income, but you cannot create a tax shelter by borrowing the money and offsetting up to $10,000 in otherwise taxable income.

The depreciation period for most real property has been extended from 19 years to 31 years, and you can no longer use accelerated depreciation, although you can use variations on the straight-line method. In the latter, you depreciate equal amounts each year, for example, $5,000 depreciated over five years would mean an annual deduction of $1,000. Accelerated depreciation brought forward to the early years the bulk of the deductions with later years' deductions much smaller. Under the old rules, you could have deducted more than three fifths of the cost of real property in less than seven years, although the depreciation period was 19 years.

These changes have meant the end to many real estate, leasing and real property tax shelters. Now, with the lower personal tax rates for individuals, many freelance professionals are trying to maximize their incomes and minimize their taxable incomes with liberal use of legitimate business deductions.

≪ THE SPECIAL CASE OF VEHICLES ≫

Tax reform further puts a crimp in the purchase and use of company vehicles. Before that trap is discussed, consider these continuing advantages of travel and vehicle deductions for the freelancer:

▶ Complete deductibility of all mileage traveled for business purposes at 22 cents per mile. If you travel 5,000 miles a year for business, that is a $1,100 deduction.

▶ Depreciation of vehicle. A corporate vehicle or vehicle used solely for business purposes can be depreciated in three years on a straight-line basis.

However, since 1984, you have had to include the full value of a company car as income to you as a corporate executive. Now, the same 2 percent AGI rule that affects personal business expenses also applies to company cars. Now, you must either keep a detailed record of how much you use a company-owned car for personal reasons, or—and an easier course—file a written statement that you are keeping records sufficient to document the car's business use. This relieves the corporation of the possibility of a problem with the IRS, and still allows the corporation to deduct the full value of the car. But it does transfer the IRS' attention to you because your statement makes you personally responsible for the records.

Furthermore, only $16,000 of the total cost of luxury cars can be depreciated, regardless of the total cost of the car. In other words, in a business where a luxury car is actually a necessity—such as brokering multimillion-dollar properties—the businessperson must absorb a great deal of that particular cost of doing business.

To avoid all of these difficulties, it may be easier to keep track of your business miles driven and take the mileage deduction to offset your actual driving costs. Of course, it would then be wise to be sure costs of the car you select can be offset at 22 cents a mile.

≪ CORPORATIONS, SOLE PROPRIETORSHIPS, PARTNERSHIPS ≫

The primary advantages of using a corporate structure for tax purposes include:

▶ Complete deductibility of reimbursable business expenses, as explained above.
▶ 100 percent deductions of medical insurance and similar fringe benefits.

▶ Protection against personal liability for the corporation's tax liabilities.

▶ Shifting the tax burden, if you take out a relatively low salary.

▶ Setting up separate corporations for spouses, in which neither spouse has an interest or position in the other spouse's corporation. This can save large sums of money on the first $50,000 of corporate profits for each corporation. The tax rate is only 15 percent. If spouses have interests in corporations together, the limit *per corporation* is $25,000.

▶ You can deduct 100 percent of the cost of many fringe benefits.

▶ You can contribute up to $7,000 to a corporate-sponsored 401(k) retirement plan while avoiding the shortcomings of other types of pension plans. Even if you work freelance part time and have a pension plan at your regular job, you can still set up a 401(k) plan through your corporate entity.

But corporations also have distinct tax disadvantages, including these:

▶ You must pay social security taxes (FICA) and withholding taxes during each pay period on your own salary and the salary of any family members which the company employs. This totals some 14.1 percent of your income.

▶ You also must pay worker's compensation for any employees, including family members.

Sole Proprietorships

Sole proprietorships offer several advantages over corporations. For example:

1. You do not have to pay FICA taxes on a spouse that you employ in the business, although you would still have to withhold income tax payments. You can avoid both FICA and income

tax payments on any wages or salary you pay your minor children up to certain limits, $3,000 during 1988. The limit increases each year, so check with your tax advisor to determine the current limits.

2. Your spouse's and family members' incomes reduce the amount of self-employment tax you have to pay. Self-employment taxes were 12.3 percent of adjusted gross income during 1987.

3. You can also sharply increase the amount you can contribute to deductible pension plans. Your spouse can set up an IRA account and deduct up to $2,000 in addition to your own contributions of up to $7,000 to a Keogh plan.

4. You may be able to file separate state tax returns and reduce your family's total state tax bill, even if you file a joint federal return. But this varies from state to state, so check it out first.

5. For the first time, a sole proprietor can deduct up to 25 percent of the cost of medical insurance premiums, and the remaining 75 percent of the cost is included in the new, much higher 7.5 percent floor of adjusted gross income for medical expenses. If you spend $1,000 on medical insurance, and earn an AGI of $30,000, the situation would be this: You could deduct $250 as a sole proprietor, but the additional $750 would be applied to an AGI floor for medical expenses of $2,250. You would need an additional $1,500 in medical expenses before you could deduct a penny more.

However, regular corporations (not Subchapter S corporations) can deduct *all* of your medical insurance costs.

Partnerships

The biggest disadvantage of a partnership is that if you set it up with a spouse, each of you has to pay 12.3 percent of your partnership profits or "draw" in FICA taxes.

The biggest advantage is that under most circumstances, you can avoid the limitations on personal business and fringe benefits deductions and deduct the full amount of all of these expenses.

The other advantage is that you can divide the losses, capital gains or losses, deductions, and tax credits in ways that do not have to directly reflect the partner's monetary or capital contribution. Thus, you can arrange a partnership to give yourself more of the deductions and credits while giving a spouse with no or lower outside income more income, which will then be taxed at lower rates than it would if it were part of your higher income.

But your tax advisor does have to fill out many more forms and schedules for partnerships and that can cost you a little more for tax return preparation.

≪ EMPLOY THE CHILDREN ≫

Although certain new rules apply to *investment* income that you arrange for your children to receive, the rules have not changed for children who work in your business. Give your children real work to do in the business and pay them reasonable wages, usually the official minimum wage for the work they can do. They can avoid withholding taxes and social security taxes on the first $3,000 of their income (in 1988, more in later years). You can even pay a child away at college to do sales, market research or any task that can be done from a distance and the same rules apply. If a 21-year-old does not go to college, the deductions stop and you can no longer avoid paying FICA taxes on his or her wages.

You can avoid taxes on an additional $2,000 of a child's income if the child puts it into an IRA account. It would remain tax-deferred until the money was withdrawn. Early withdrawals from IRA plans, except for specifically allowed purposes, carry stiff penalties, but a child may want to use the IRA as a nest egg after he or she leaves college and gets married and may be willing to bear the penalty.

≪ HOME IS WHERE THE SHELTER IS ≫

An office at home can provide more than one kind of shelter. It can also be a very good tax shelter. Part-time freelancers must be very careful about offices at home. The IRS could contend that your freelance work is a hobby, or not intended to make a profit and might then disallow any office at home deductions. To avoid this, either register a business name or incorporate, if the additional costs and hassles are adequately offset by the anticipated office-at-home deductions. This step, and actively doing business, usually signals the IRS that you are serious.

If your office at home is your *sole* place of business, you will have no trouble taking very significant deductions. You can deduct a proportional amount of your rent or mortgage principal, property taxes, utilities, basic telephone service, cost of repairs, and directly related maintenance (lawn care services are not usually deductible), depreciation, even security systems and services.

The proportion of these costs that you can deduct are generally determined in one of two ways:

1. *By room.* If you live in a five-room house, and one of those rooms is used *exclusively* for business purposes, you can deduct 20 percent of the above costs, or one-fifth of your costs.

2. *By square footage.* Suppose your house has seven rooms and 1,500 square feet, but your office takes up 400 square feet of space. Under the room method, you would deduct about 14 percent. Using the square-foot method, you would deduct about 27 percent of the costs.

The IRS is very strict about these rules, and has challenged many office-at-home deductions over the years. But by and large, the deductions hold firm for freelancers, working either full- or part-time. Although this book is not directly concerned with such situations, you can deduct an office at home if your employer makes it a job requirement or condition of employment. But you cannot deduct office at home expenses if you buy and sell stocks or act as a private investor.

Professionals facing difficulty include college professors because conflicting court cases have both upheld and denied their office-at-home deductions. By mid-1987, their status had not yet been clarified by an appeals court decision.

The technical rules governing this area state that you can deduct certain expenses *only if* that part of your home is used *regularly and exclusively* as your principal place of business for any trade or business; a meeting place for patients, clients, or customers in the normal course of business; or a separate structure not attached to your residence; or the use must be for the convenience of your employer and not just helpful to you in your work. You could run three different businesses out of two rooms of your house and a freestanding building, and deduct the costs related to all three if they meet these requirements.

Office-at-Home Exceptions

One beneficial exception to the rules concerns storage space. You can deduct part of your garage or basement if you use that part exclusively and continuously for storage.

Yet, your total office-at-home deduction cannot exceed the gross income you earn by working at home. This is a definite tax trap. You must first deduct from your gross income the amount you claim for office-at-home expenses before you apply any other deductions. If the total office deductions equal or exceed your gross income, you cannot deduct any other expenses and take a tax loss against other personal or family income. For example, suppose you earned a gross income of $10,000 in your at-home business, but you could legitimately deduct $15,000 for at-home expenses. You could only deduct $10,000 and eliminate any current tax obligations, but you could not apply the $5,000 difference to your spouse's or family's income from other jobs or businesses.

The IRS also applies a formula to the division of these expenses. For example, suppose you can deduct 20 percent of your home expenses based on the use of your home for your business, and you had a gross income of $1,000 from your business. The at-home expenses are divided this way:

	Total	Portion
1. Taxes	$1,500	$ 300
2. Mortgage interest	2,000	400
3. Operating expenses	1,000	200
4. Depreciation	3,000	600
TOTAL	$7,500	$1,500

But your income was only $1,000. The deductions would be applied like this: all $300 for taxes, all $400 for interest and all $200 for operating expenses, but only $100 of the total for depreciation. However, if your income was very low, and you had left over tax and mortgage interest portions, you could still deduct them on your Schedule A itemized return, preserving these deductions. You can, however, lose all or part of your operating expense and depreciation deductions.

You can deduct all of the costs of painting and repairing existing rooms, but you cannot deduct the cost of *remodeling, renovating or restoring* a room. Yet, you can deduct part of the cost of painting the outside of the house or repairing heating and air conditioning, plumbing and water systems that serve the whole house as well as the roof.

The changes in these rules have made them more arcane than ever, and somewhat harder to use. But you should still take full advantage of these rules when you begin because they can help boost your profits—or even your ability to keep going—in the early days.

The Home Computer Mess

Deducting the cost of home computers for employees is a complex situation governed by strict rules. However, if you own a home-based freelance business, and you use a personal computer almost exclusively for business (you can play games on it occasionally), you will have no difficulty deducting its full cost under the $10,000 exclusionary rule, or depreciating the cost. But do not try to deduct a personal computer that is kept in a different part of the house, or one that Junior uses most of the time for school work, or playing games. If you do not use the computer in your freelance business, but use it at least 50 percent of the time for investment analysis, you can still depreciate or deduct the cost under a different set of rules not related to starting a freelance business. In general, however, you do best to simply treat a personal computer like any ordinary piece of office equipment.

≪ RETIREMENT PLAN ADVANTAGES ≫

As briefly noted, freelance professionals can take maximum advantage of various kinds of retirement plans depending on their income and circumstances. If you have a corporation, you can set up a "nonqualified" plan and contribute almost as much as you want to it. If you are a sole proprietor or act in a partnership, you can deduct up to $7,000 a year through a Keogh plan. If you are a part-time freelancer, you can choose either the higher limits of the Keogh or the lower $2,000 limit of the IRA plan. (If you are employed, but your company does not offer a "qualified" pension plan, you can still contribute $2,000 to an IRA and deduct that amount from your taxes.) If your wife and children work for you, they, too, can start their own IRA plans. So, under normal circumstances, you can contribute $9,000 yourself, and $2,000 each for family members you employ.

There are many complex details about retirement planning and taxes, so consult your tax advisor before you set up a plan.

Basically, a Keogh plan is a retirement savings vehicle for self-employed professionals in sole proprietorships, partnerships or "S" corporations through which you can contribute (and deduct) up to $7,000 of your gross adjusted income each year to a retirement fund. A 401(k) Plan is a different vehicle through which a "C" corporation can establish a retirement plan for all of its employees. It allows the corporation to make deductible contributions to the retirement plan in amounts that can depend on an employee's status and income. The corporation can contribute far more dollars for executives than for secretaries, and in some cases, it even allows for different classes of contributions for different kinds of employees.

See the extensive listing of books and articles on retirement planning in the resource section of this book for more information on this complex subject.

≪ You Have to Pay to Play ≫

Although most freelance professionals are very adept at taking advantage of tax deductions, many fail to fulfill the filing requirements and suffer steep penalties. The new law makes these penalties much harsher than they used to be, too.

Here is a list of the essential forms and filing dates for federal income and FICA tax returns:

▶ W-4 forms for each employee to determine the number of exemptions each wants. Filled out and filed when you employ someone.

▶ W-2 forms which show the total annual wages, salaries and bonuses of each employee along with the amount of withholding taxes each has already paid. They must be filed and copies given to each employee by January 31 of each year for the preceding calendar year.

▶ Form 1099-B which any client that pays you $600 or more each year must file, listing all of the income paid to you during the preceding calendar year. By January 31 of each year.

▶ Form 1040, the long tax form and accompanying schedules. By April 15, unless you file a Form 4868 and ask for an extension until August 1 or October 1.

▶ Form 1040 Schedules:

Schedule A, Itemized Deductions

Schedule C, Profit or (Loss) from Business or Profession, for sole proprietors

Schedule D, Capital Gains and Losses and Reconciliation of Forms 1099-B

Schedule E, Supplemental Income Schedule

Schedule SE, Computation of Social Security Self-Employment Tax

Form 2106, Employee Business Expenses

Form 3903, Moving Expenses (for sole proprietors)

Form 4562, Depreciation and Amortization

Form 4797, Gains and Losses from Sales or Exchanges of Assets Used in a Trade or Business and Involuntary Conversions

▶ Form 1065, a partnership return, one for each partnership in which you participate.

Corporations must file similar rafts of forms that apply to their particular circumstances. A CPA is a must for most of these.

Payment Deadlines

You also should make a habit of making your quarterly income tax, FICA, withholding and worker's compensation payments on time to avoid the onerous penalties. The worst is a flat 9 percent of the total owed, plus continuing interest charges at a relatively high rate. This interest is added on top of the penalty charges, too.

Payment deadlines for freelance professionals include:

▶ April 15 for both quarterly tax payments for the quarter ended March 31, and for filing of annual tax returns and payment of taxes due.

▶ July 15, for quarterly return and payment of taxes for quarter ended June 30.

▶ October 15, for quarterly returns and payment of taxes for quarter ended September 30. Also last day for filing of tax returns for which a Form 4868 had been filed.

▶ January 15, for quarterly tax returns and payment of taxes for quarter ended December 31.

You can choose a different fiscal year and file your final tax returns of the year according to that fiscal year, but you must still make quarterly payments and file returns according to a similar quarterly schedule. You must file a Form 1128, Application for Change in Accounting Period, to change your fiscal years to anything other than a calendar year.

Despite the complexity of many of these points, keep in mind that working as a freelance professional gives you far more control over your tax situation than most employees ever have. This freedom to maximize your legitimate deductions and to make quarterly payments instead of having money withheld from your paycheck every week can improve your cash flow and put your money to work for your business purposes, not the federal government's. A freelance business of your own is truly the last great tax shelter for the middle class.

≪ 7 ≫

HOW CAN YOU GET—
AND KEEP—THE BUSINESS?

You find and keep clients and generate new ones with a steady, consistent plan to promote your service and yourself. You should never let your efforts falter because a competitor always waits in the wings, if not at the client's door, to take your place—and your fees. And your "market," the group of clients or executives and managers that you serve, constantly changes. Clients change jobs (creating an opportunity, too); you may follow the client to his or her new job, but retain your favorable position with the new person in the client's old job. The new person may often need your help to learn the ropes and make a smooth transition. It would be a mistake to assume that the "new broom" wants to sweep clean. If you assume that you want to work with the new person, and act accordingly, you usually can establish a new relationship rather easily.

On the other hand, clients die, get married, stop working, change industries, or go through prolonged personal or business difficulties. For no apparent reason, they may feel like changing freelancers. They may want to try a new approach. Their companies' fortunes may change for the worse. Practically anything can happen to disrupt a relationship, or prevent you from establishing a relationship. A steady, consistent sales and promotion effort is your only protection against these changes in the winds of fortune.

Yet, if you maintain good relations and perform quality service, they will still think well of you, and refer business to you when they get the opportunity. For example, an important client of mine changed business emphases and no longer required my services. But almost a year later, my former client referred a Fortune 500 company to me for market research work that my former client could not do, but he knew that I could.

≪ PRINCIPLES OF PROMOTION ≫

The principles of selling and promoting freelance services are few and simple.

Discover and Serve Client Needs

First and most important, you should discover your client's needs. This topic was discussed in some detail in Chapter 5, but it bears repeating here. If you offer a limited range of services, as any independent freelancer must, you must take one or both of two actions:

1. Find the available buyers for your services with a diligent search. This is the function of your preliminary market survey. You wanted them to at least identify where you could find potential clients. Now, take the next step and actively seek out those who may need your services.
2. Act flexibly and offer the services, within your field or a field in which you can participate, that the most, best, largest, best paying, or highest quality clients *need*. Fish take the bait they like to eat, not the bait a fisherman wants to lure them with. You don't fish for rainbow trout with shark chum; you use

colorful, attractive flies that look like flying insects, a trout's favorite food. Clients act the same in that they want what they want and they will not "bite" at anything foreign to their business palates.

Usually, you will combine the two to mix your services as well as you can to match clients' needs. One successful market researcher started out as a freelance writer. He knew the basics of market research because he had done some election polling for regional newspapers and local political candidates. After a high-technology firm read some of his work on microcomputers, the firm called and offered him market research work. If the freelancer had followed path 1, he would have refused the work, saying it was not in his field. But since he believed in himself, knew the basics, and felt he could learn the rest, he followed path 2, and established a very profitable, long-term relationship with the firm.

This may seem to contradict earlier statements about going with strengths and avoiding weaknesses. But it does not because the fledgling market researcher did not know whether he could do the work or not. He had never been asked before, but he felt he knew the basics well from his previous experience in political polling. And he was determined to try because the field promised to be very lucrative. He experimented and found that market research was an untapped *strength.* If he had experimented and found he did poor quality research, he would have acted unwisely if he continued to pursue more market research clients after an initial bad experience.

Define Your Product

Even if you have to take seminars or refresher courses to fill in gaps of knowledge, you should offer services within related fields as broad as your basic knowledge or willingness to learn will allow. Yet, you cannot be all things to all people, or you scatter your efforts and waste your energies. You should first define your product in these terms:

▸ Services you can offer or you could offer in the near future.

▸ The personality, reputation and image you want to convey.

▸ The quality and reliability you wish to provide.

In fact, you should understand that any freelance professional works in the same way that a custom "job shop" operates. You offer customized services that meet a client's needs. You very rarely would offer the same product to millions of buyers like a soap or auto manufacturer. Rather, you tailor your service to each client, and you must "individualize" your approach to each.

Let Your Clients Shape Your Services

Ask potential clients what they need, what they want, how you can satisfy them, how you should adapt your planned services, how much they pay now or are willing to pay, do they need any new services, what kinds of services they would like to get if they were available. Ask, discuss, and above all, *listen*. Then, *refine* your services to match those most strongly desired by the clients most likely to buy and pay the best price. This may not be the largest company; they may have large staffs that already provide the bulk of the services you offer. Or they may hire large consulting firms that can offer a range and depth of services that you cannot match. But, you can approach large companies with these selling concepts:

▸ It is a bad idea for them to rely on just one service or consultant. They should hire you as a reliable second opinion or "second source" of freelance services.

▸ Encourage them to call on you when their staff is too busy to take on small or emergency jobs. You can fill in the gap for them and make handsome, or at least, higher than usual fees if you play the role of "clean-up hitter," or "bail-out specialist." If you can deliver quality work by cleaning up other people's mistakes and messes, you can do very well in any freelance business.

▶ Be careful and avoid only taking on the worst, most difficult jobs. Some freelancers complain that they only get the "bears" that their clients do not want to handle themselves. To mix metaphors, it will be hard to smell the roses, i.e., work at the smaller, easier projects, if you are always shoveling manure.

However, one freelancer who enjoyed the challenge went out of her way to become known as a "bail-out specialist." She took on the worst jobs at the very last minute for dozens of clients. Why? Not particularly because she liked to work hard under constant deadline pressure. Rather, she liked the premium fees, double the normal fees, that taming the "bears" earned her. So, it is your choice, but a good mix of bail-out work and regular contracts can increase your income and smooth out peaks and valleys in your cash flow.

≪ CHOOSE YOUR "LOCATION" CAREFULLY ≫

You also need to decide where your market is, in geographic terms. Ask whether or not you can reach a nationwide audience, or must limit your services to a regional or local market. Management consultants, freelance writers, and the like can use telephones, overnight delivery, and air transportation to serve their clients from anywhere in the country—if they have or can gather the information a distant client requires. It is easier to offer national companies national freelance services because they, too, want to reach a national audience. You can also travel fairly frequently to let your clients know that you remain very interested in serving them. Otherwise, as mentioned earlier, you could experience the "out of sight, out of mind" problem unless you use other means of staying in close touch.

Otherwise, if your potential clients are clustered in one area, as the auto manufacturers are located in or around Michigan and the Midwestern states, you would do best to locate your business near them. Once you have established an excellent reputation, you may be able to live where you want to, but you can lose that reputation if you do not continue to "press the flesh," as politicians might say. Although I live in Florida, I still make several trips a year to New York to visit with my editors and publishers and I stay in frequent contact with my leading clients by phone on a regular basis. Out of sight, out of mind is a truism in any freelance business. In short, go where your market takes you. You have to be a rarity for the market to chase you.

≪ SUPERIORITY DOESN'T ALWAYS SUCCEED ≫

The second principle is that even if you provide high quality services and superior knowledge, you still may not gain clients unless your clients hear about your virtues, come to appreciate them, and hear about them again and again. Successful selling and promotion are based on telling the truth, but putting the best possible light on that truth.

To succeed, you need to combine a good package of services, be in the right place at the right time, charge reasonable fees, and present an attractive, appealing, appropriate professional image based on your own personality.

≪ ACT DIFFERENTLY ≫

The second promotion principle is: Analyze the competition and then offer something different. It could be a new niche, your specialized knowledge, skills or talents, your reliability for on-time delivery, the quality of your work, unique information you have developed, a unique business theory or method of doing business, anything that distinguishes you from the competition. Then, as you'll learn at the end of the chapter, promote this difference again and again.

You must consistently know your competition very well before you can establish a unique identity. For quick competitive research, attend trade shows, talk to potential clients, join professional associations, congregate—occasionally—where competitors go. Observe, listen, and analyze. Look for ways to take a different, although equally or even more valid approach.

▶ *Company name.* One of the author's favorite business names is that of an Irish law firm, Argue and Phibb. Yes, it really exists in County Sligo in the Republic of Ireland. And those are the lawyers' real names. So, a catchy company name must be appropriate to the field, but have a large grain of truth to it.

▶ *Company image.* Use attractive, eye-catching brochures, logos, business cards, stationery, direct mail pieces. Be sure that they, too, are appropriate to your service and field. For example, a belly dancer might profitably use photographic business cards, but they might be inappropriate for a CPA who wants corporate clients.

▶ *Consistent image.* Make sure that your image is consistent. Carry it through not only your printed materials, but also your personal appearance, the style and quality of your presentations and proposals, and so forth. If you want to establish a reputation and image for reliability in a field where freelancers are notoriously unreliable, dress conservatively, use gray or off white, high quality business papers, adopt a straight-forward and forthright attitude. On the other hand, if you want to convey a "flaky" image, use colored stationery, send outrageous notes, pull off-the-wall stunts, etc. But then dress and act the part, too.

For example, freelance writers as a group tend to have a flaky image and a reputation for being undependable. So, at a time when most male freelance writers clunked around in boots, flannel shirts and cowboy hats, and most female writers dressed like leftover hippies, I dressed in conservative, well-tailored business suits, wore silk ties, walked in polished shoes, and carried a leather briefcase. I used grey business stationery and adopted a business name that read like the name of a firm of conservative lawyers. All of this, plus working hard and producing quality work, quickly established the positive image that I wanted to convey. Of course, that image was contrary to the negative image that the publishing industry tends to place on most freelance writers.

≪ REPUTATION: YOUR GREATEST ASSET OR WEAKEST LINK ≫

Your image and personality begin to establish your reputation. Remember that reputation reflects other people's *perception* of you and your firm. It may not reflect what you think of yourself, but you must do all you can to establish the reputation you want—consider The Rolling Stones' reputation as the bad boys of rock, yet some of them appear to have become caring parents. But don't tell their fans that; their record sales might go down. Then, support that reputation and reinforce it with a coordinated effort.

Reputations are built in the worst possible way: by word of mouth through gossip, attitudes, body language, and hints of perception shared between two people. Others' opinions of you always become part of your reputation, despite any promotion or publicity you can otherwise place. Remember the worm scare that threatened the reputation of a large hamburger franchise, or the devil symbol scare that threatened a leading consumer goods company? Most people do, despite the obvious falseness of the allegations. That is how fragile your reputation can be.

The best ingredient in establishing a reputation is not what you *want* other people to think of you, but your attitude toward yourself and others. If you consistently maintain a positive, upbeat, helpful, caring, and professional attitude tempered with cautious optimism and "humility," in the good sense of the term, you can gain and reap the rewards of a good reputation. Even an eccentric "character" can maintain a good reputation if his or her eccentricities are benevolent and benefit the client.

In general, since most freelancers work with managers in large companies, you need to present a humble and hardworking attitude. You need to emphasize that you want a client's business and that you are eager to serve. In all seriousness, how could you expect to act arrogantly or with a haughty air of superiority toward a client and have that client respond in a subordinate or servile manner? Even the thought is ludicrous. You are the one who wants the work, so express your willingness to do it. Make clients feel good about using your services. Keep up a regular flow of notes, clippings, telephone calls, and appropriate gifts to show your clients how much you appreciate them. In sum, consistently high quality performance, combined with a quality and appropriate "personality," attracts and keeps clients. But how do you find new clients in the first place?

≪ FINDING NEW CLIENTS ≫

First, you start close to home in your own company or among your contacts in your industry who already have a high opinion of your work. This can be risky, especially if you fail to perform up to expectations on your first assignments. You can do irreparable harm if you disappoint your friends. It may be better to establish some new clients before you approach old friends. Or just use old friends for referrals to other prospects. Remember that your first *satisfied* customer is your best customer.

Next, obtain referrals from friends in noncompetitive companies before you leave your company, or to obtain part-time assignments. People are usually willing to help a friend launch a new venture, especially if their help reflects well on them.

Third, closely review trade and related business publications to find out about people who change jobs, new managers in companies and positions of direct interest to you, new companies that may need your services, old contacts that have resurfaced in new companies, companies that are seeking the services you can offer, and so forth.

Fourth, when you identify potential clients, take one of two approaches, dictated by your experience, desire and selling techniques common to the field:

1. Call and establish contact with the highest level decision-maker that can hire you to do the work. Making cold calls to

strangers is tough, but you can pre-qualify prospects by checking with friends to see if that person is known to them. If they don't know the person, persist and make the call anyway. Check into the person's or company's background and current situation so you can speak intelligently about what you might be able to offer. You'd be surprised at how many freelancers have no idea what a company does or makes, yet they try to sell their services by making cold—and ignorant— sales calls to easily annoyed managers. These managers surely will not hire you if you do not even know basic information about their companies.

For example, one freelance editor worked with a new small publisher to help him go through more than 200 manuscripts and book proposals that had accumulated during the transition. Although the publisher had *never* published fiction, the editor found not one or two, but almost a dozen proposals or manuscripts for works of fiction. Even more surprisingly, most of them had come from literary agents. This means that none of the agents or writers had bothered to find out what kind of books that the publisher wanted to buy. Their effort, time, and expense were wasted by their own laziness. Simply looking up the publisher in *The Literary Marketplace* or *The Writer's Market* would have told them what they needed to know. So, look before you leap; simple, but too often overlooked.

2. Or write the person a personal note with a clipping or information of interest. Include an attractive brochure that describes your services. Then follow up with a telephone call and a request for an appointment so you can discuss the person's needs.

Telemarketing Techniques for Freelancers

Telemarketing yourself as a freelance professional by telephone can be the best and quickest way to contact potential clients. Several books and articles cited in the resource section can help you develop these techniques, but the best approach is that generally followed by stockbrokers: You make the person an offer they can not afford not to listen to. Most stockbrokers spend 10 to 12 hours a day on the phone prospecting for new clients for whom to trade stocks or bonds. They find these prospects through lists of affluent individuals and executives, and they have a prepared presentation that they follow designed to attract each person's attention, usually a "hot" stock or bond deal that they want the person to buy.

You have to be more subtle, but the concept is the same:

Pre-qualify your potential clients. Know before you call that the person you want to reach may need your services. Remember the example of the ignorant literary agents above. If you only think someone may need your service, first call an assistant or subordinate and ask, for example: "Does your company ever use packaging consultants to help you design new boxes for your cereals?" If the answer is even something like, "Well, once in a blue moon," you have an opening. Only if the answer is "absolutely never" do you accept the answer as final—for awhile. Call back in a month or two, and see if the situation has changed.

You can also use the preliminary call to find out who the key executive decisionmaker—at least the person who hires consultants—is, if you do not already know. Ask the person to whom you speak, call other individuals within the company, ask the public relations or personnel department, but do anything to find the decisionmaker before you call.

Get through the gatekeeper. If the answer is even a tentative yes, then call the key executive. Getting through a well-trained secretary to speak with the executive is both an art and a skill. Usually, at first, you cannot, unless you have some offer of such immediate or unusual need that you overcome the secretary's fine-honed resistance. You can't say, "Ms. So-and-So, I have an offer that Mr. Smith can't refuse. Put him on the phone."

Instead, you take a conversational approach, explaining your purpose. You need to treat assistants and secretaries with great respect. They are the gatekeepers, and they can make smooth your path, or make it impossible for your calls to get through. If you have a reference to Mr. Smith from a friend or colleague of his, name-drop it all over the secretary: "Ms. So-and-So, Mr. Jones at BMI Corp. suggested that I get in touch with Mr. Smith right away. Could I speak with Mr. Smith, please?"

By the way, the most effective gate-openers are the old stand-bys—please and thank you—and a courteous, respectful, and charming tone of voice.

Usually, you have to play "telephone tag" with your potential client because most people are either very busy, on the road, in meetings, or avoiding you. The only secrets are persistence—and establishing a relationship with the gatekeeper. Every time you call, gently probe and ask specifically when the executive can be reached. Ask what the best times to call back might be. Make sure you leave the best times for you to be called back. If an occasion arises to compliment the secretary for being helpful, having a nice voice, treating you courteously, and so on, be very generous in your thanks and praise.

TIP: I have tried with some success the opposite of the courteous approach. I have called some firms and said, in effect, "This is Robert Laurance of (My-Firm-Name). Could I speak with Mr. Smith, please" with some degree of firmness in my voice. Occasionally, the firmness will make the secretary respond and put me right through to the manager. I do not have any rules of thumb about when this approach works. I have learned to rely on my intuition and the reputation of the company or executive (if I know it) before I call. If you try this approach and it doesn't work, immediately switch to the courteous approach.

Go straight to the point. When you reach the executive, introduce yourself and your purpose. Give a sentence or two of your background and accomplishments, and then succinctly describe the services that you offer. Preferably, you will know what service the potential client may need before you call. For example, I found a new magazine for which I became interested in writing. I reviewed its contents and developed two ideas that I thought the editor might like. I called three times before I got through to the editor. I said, in effect, "My name is Robert Laurance. I have written many articles and profiles of high-tech corporate managers like those you publish. In fact, I have just prepared several chapters of a new book based on interviews with (names of several leading high-tech executives). And I have a couple of ideas for you."

I had quickly and effectively captured the editor's interest. I then described my ideas, and she said that she liked them. She added that I was definitely the type of experienced writer with whom she wanted to work. Then, I knew I had an excellent shot at an assignment. She asked me to send samples and a brief outline of the idea. I did so, and subsequently, I received an assignment that enabled me to make my first trip to Boston, expenses paid, and I earned a good fee for the article. I enjoyed doing the work, and I got paid fairly quickly.

In general, this example is how most freelance professionals can best use telephone selling techniques. You should never sound like you are selling vacuum cleaners by phone. Never make your "spiel" sound canned or prepared. I had probably said the same thing that I said to that editor to a dozen other editors, but I did not read it. I just talked about my work and how I believed my services could fulfill her magazine's requirements.

If she had not been in the market for that service, I was equally prepared to ask her what kind of editorial services or requirements she had. I was prepared to react flexibly to match what I could do with what she wanted. Of course, I already knew from preliminary research that my experience would match at least one of her editorial needs.

Be prepared, too, for your telephone selling to only open the door. You will rarely get a firm commitment on your first phone call. Usually, you will need to follow up with a written proposal or personal presentation, and have more discussions with the decisionmaker. You will have to sell your experience, skills, talents, and personality to win new contracts.

Best of all, this approach is relatively inexpensive. In the example, the telephone calls cost about $10, the mailing less than $2, the copies about $2. So, for about $20 in selling costs, plus my time, I received an assignment that netted me a profit several dozen times greater than my out-of-pocket costs.

In short, a well-prepared and personable telephone presentation can be your most effective, least expensive, and most rewarding technique to find "hot" new prospects.

Build a mailing list of prospects. Once or twice a year, send everyone on it a sales letter and brochure. This can help overcome the "out of sight, out of mind" problem. You would be pleasantly surprised at how many managers keep brochures on file and refer to them when a need arises. By the way, people are more likely to keep and refer to attractive and interesting brochures than business cards. An unusual postcard appropriate to your field can be memorable as well.

You need not do an expensive, four-color brochure with photographs, unless you are an artist, or someone in an exotic field where that approach would help. Many freelance professionals, such as writers and editors, even engineers, may want to use a printed vita of accomplishments supported by samples and letters of reference. Others, such as management consultants, may want to do a two-color brochure. If you do a brochure, make it look professionally designed. Avoid dark or unusual color papers. Use paper that folds easily. You can use a brochure with one fold and four panels, or a two-fold, six-panel brochure equally well. If you use a quick printing shop to design, lay out, typeset, and print the brochure, you can expect to pay $150 to $300 for 500 to 1,000 brochures.

Mail out the brochures in attractive envelopes. You can save money by using regular No. 10 business envelopes for both letters and brochures. If you feel you need something unique or unusual, use a four-page 8 ¹/₂ by 11 brochure that fits into a regular 9 by 12 envelope. Keep the total weight to one or two ounces to save postage costs. Always send letters and brochures with "First Class" prominently stamped on the envelope. This simple step shows clients that you think they are worthy of first-class treatment. Most second class or third class mail gets thrown into the garbage. At your level, executives are used to and expect first class treatment, especially in their own domains.

Normal business stationery, in 1,000-piece lots, costs between $50 and $300, depending on the paper quality, layout, typesetting, and printer's charges.

You can expect a 1,000-piece mailing to cost between $650 and $1,000, depending on whether you pay an assistant or part-time help to type addresses on envelopes, or you do it yourself or with your family's help.

How do you develop a mailing list? Start with your own address book or file of telephone numbers and addresses. Then use industry directories, association membership lists, trade publications, business telephone directories, or any source of exact names, titles, company names and addresses. Getting a potential client's name, title, company, and address spelled correctly is very, very important. Do not overlook these details. I lost a bid for a lucrative public relations contract one time because the company president did not like typographical errors in proposals, and mine had three.

TIP: Should you use some eye-catching or attention-getting message on a direct mail piece? Unless it is a news release or something of vital interest to your prospects, I advise against it. A personal, first-class letter in attractive, professional stationery with a brochure and personalized letter written to the executive obtains better results in my experience. You are not selling executive toys by mail, but a serious service.

Seek out the toughest, most difficult-to-see prospects. Persist because your competitors are far less likely to overcome their doubts and inability to reach the decisionmakers.

Identify prospects' special requirements and appeal to their need to satisfy them. Remember that accepting emergency assignments, handling overflow from a busy department, and acting as a "second source" can dramatically improve your business. Ask the key executive's secretary, assistant, or subordinates what special requirements he or she may have.

Offer a line or package of services. Encourage the client to pick and choose what he or she needs. But offer discount prices if they buy the whole package. I do not write only books and magazine articles. I also write market research reports, speeches, public relations releases, advertising copy, editorial material for advertising supplements, and more. Frankly, I could not reach my desired level of success with just one or two of these, but I can and do working in all of them.

Knock on doors and make "cold calls." Get your foot in the door with interesting techniques, such as sending handwritten notes in to a manager that say something like, "Dear Ms. Jones, Would you like to know how you can save $5,000 a month in personnel costs with no investment?" This approach may not work every time, but it will certainly grab Ms. Jones' attention. However, when you make cold calls, cluster your visits in a concentrated area so you make the best use of your limited time and transportation dollars. Then, follow up these notes with telephone calls. The notes give you an immediate "in" and a topic of conversation. You can ask the secretary whether or not the executive received and read the note. If the executive received the note favorably, he or she will be more likely to accept or return your phone call.

This approach has worked for me many times. When I see something good written or broadcast about a potential client, I send a note and follow up with a call within several days. For example, I recently wanted to sell market research services to a new client in a new market segment. I heard that the prospect was taking a unique approach in his industry. And I saw it mentioned in a national publication. I copied the clipping and sent a note of congratulations, and a description of my services. I followed up with several phone calls, and I was given the opportunity to make a presentation. At this writing, I had not received a contract, but my chances for obtaining something were very good. This is just one example of how the personal note has proven very effective.

Emphasize these points: you will want to help the client save money, improve productivity, fill a gaping hole in his operations or knowledge, or satisfy an unmet need. Sell personal helpfulness, not just your services. Offer, suggest, recommend, and give ideas all for free in addition to your services. In short, add value to your basic services.

Finally, persist, persist, persist. When someone says no, send a note thanking them for their consideration. Within a short time, send another note or make another call as long as you have something new or interesting to give the prospect. Tickle, remind, inform, congratulate, take note of new products, do whatever is appropriate and professional to keep your name in the forefront of that person's mind.

Then, when you meet with the client, always show the courtesy of asking for the sale. People like to be asked to buy. And when a client gives you a freelance assignment, show your appreciation with a thank you note. Tell the client how much you appreciate his business and how much you think of him and his company. Remind him that you think he has made the right choice, not only to reinforce his good feeling, but to help the client get over the "hump" of doubt that tends to creep into client's minds. Most people are tempted to second-guess their decisions. But your continuing follow-through will eliminate that doubt before it has a chance to grow.

≪ SETTING PRICES AND FEES ≫

You set your prices or fees according to several factors: current fee schedules; needed profit margins; and clients' ability to pay. You rarely have the chance to establish a new price structure because someone somewhere has offered a similar service before. However, you do not necessarily have to offer fees lower than your competition to get the business. In fact, in freelancing, clients worry that they will receive poor quality service if they pay less than they think the service is worth. You can also charge premium prices for special services because the client's perceived value of those services is greater. You can offer added value to your services to maintain a price level in the face of tough competition. You also use promotion, publicity, and reputation to raise your prices. A freelancer with a national reputation gets paid more than one with strictly local recognition.

I have had local magazine editors apologize to me for paying what they thought were low fees for articles. My response is usually: "I've been paid very little and I've been paid an awful lot. I want to work with you, and your fee schedule is adequate for this assignment." What they didn't know—and I wasn't about to tell them—was that their article fees were higher than that paid by many national magazines.

If you offer or accept a discounted fee, explain why you are willing to do so: help out a valued client who has a budget problem, establish good will with a new customer, want to work in a new and interesting area, and so forth.

You may run into a situation where the fee is just too low to accept, and you have to turn down an assignment. When would that occur? If you consider the work involved and conclude that the expenses will equal or exceed the fee, do not accept the assignment, except in one or two exceptional circumstances. If the assignment gives you experience in a new field you very seriously want to enter, do it, so you can use the experience to expand your presence in that field. If a valued client asks you to do the job as a favor, and it does not take too long, then do it to maintain a relationship and put him in a position where he owes you a favor.

It may turn out that unforeseen circumstances mean that your expenses exceed your fees: a client refuses to pay the agreed upon fee, and offers you a settlement for less; your car breaks down on the way to an interview; an airline loses your luggage during a trip, and the reimbursement and your insurance, plus the fee, do not cover the replacement cost of what you lost; your work is rejected the first time, and you have to re-do it, spending more time and money; or you simply have to make more phone calls and more trips, do more research and more work than you anticipated. I have done work that paid less than $1 an hour, and I have done work that paid $500 an hour. You should not get hung up over whether you earn an exact hourly fee every hour of every day. You won't. You need to consider your overall rate of return.

To do this, divide the number of hours you work per month by your *net income* after you subtract expenses, but before you subtract your personal, family, and living expenses. For example, if you work 160 hours one month (4 weeks at 40 hours a week), and earn $5,000 that month, your gross hourly rate is $31.25 per hour. If you have $1,000 in expenses, then your net income is $4,000 and a rate of $25 per hour.

≪ CONSIDER PROFIT MARGINS ≫

More important than net income and hourly rates are your actual net profits and profit margin. The rule of thumb among accountants and professionals is that a freelance professional, or any personal service business, should earn a *net profit margin* before personal expenses between 50 and 70 percent. Of course, the higher the better. So, your business expenses should not exceed 30 to 50 percent of your gross income. For example, if your gross income is $50,000, your expenses should not exceed $15,000 to $25,000 for you to retain adequate funds for living expenses.

In many cases, your personal and business expenses may blend together, and getting an accurate picture may be hard. Keep careful records of business expenses, and you can usually get an accurate idea of how much you are making. If your expenses begin to exceed the range cited above, you can rest assured that your personal lifestyle will begin to suffer, and you will need to either reduce your business expenses or obtain more clients.

≪ USE PUBLICITY AND PROMOTION JUDICIOUSLY ≫

One of the best ways to maintain or increase your fees is to establish a national or high-profile reputation and name recognition. Gary Carter, All-Star catcher for the New York Mets, gets more money to endorse a product than a minor leaguer. The same principle applies in the freelance business. Delivering high quality work will do this, but slowly. So, use basic publicity techniques to enhance your reputation and name recognition.

This promotion must fit the circumstances. A very inexpensive, yet consistently successful way is to make yourself *the* expert in your field. Send out press releases to trade journals and relevant and important newspapers and magazines on a regular basis. Use them to reveal the results of new research, propose dramatic new theories, report on the results of surveys, identify important new trends, or present any information that editors might consider "newsworthy."

You could contribute articles and columns to leading trade publications. You could cultivate a relationship with key journalists and editors in the field.

Serve on panels, committees, forums, conference boards, and the like for the exposure to potential clients and to do your own market and competitive research. Submit academic papers to journals and conference proceedings. Give speeches to key trade associations or professional groups. Place all of these activities and information in the right media.

One very successful promotional technique is the free information service to clients. Every month or quarter, send to everyone on your mailing list or a mailing list of key decisionmakers and publications and news media an information report. It could be any of these:

▶ Market surveys, updated and explored.
▶ Trends analysis.
▶ New technologies and their impact.
▶ Impact of government actions.

▶ On-going surveys of business activities, such as company plans to hire new employees, build new plants, etc.

Anything that gives prospects and the media something to think about. Then, use these information reports and copies of articles, speeches, proceedings and the like as marketing tools.

One very successful example of these steps also shows how revenge can spur one to success as a professional freelancer. In 1972, a high-technology market researcher was owed many thousands of dollars for not one, but *six* market research reports by a leading—and still very prominent—national market research firm. The firm would not pay the researcher. But he had to eat and feed his kids, so he decided to get even and make some money by competing with his former client. He developed a mailing list from his own contacts in the field, and he sent out several thousand solicitations for his reports to the people on that list. And he charged a high price for his detailed, often controversial reports, a price at which he knew he could make a healthy profit.

At the same time, he sent out press releases to trade publications, and actively courted the editors and reporters at both the trade papers and such prominent publications as *The Wall Street Journal* and *The New York Times*. The result? He received enough orders not only to eat and pay his bills, but to establish a foundation for his own market research publishing firm. Since then, he has become and remained very successful, often employing as many as 30 people at a time.

Then he assiduously promoted himself as *the* expert in markets for various high technology products and industries for years. He began to be quoted in practically every issue of pertinent trade journals. One trade journal even used him in an advertisement promoting subscriptions to the publication. He was asked to appear at conferences and sit on panels so often that he began to turn them down, or charge high fees. Yet, he kept up a steady stream of new reports and press releases, and began publishing several newsletters, all designed to build on his growing reputation.

Within a few years, he had succeeded well enough to commission the construction of the sailboat of his dreams, pay for both of his children to attend Ivy League schools simultaneously, and live in the style to which he wished to remain accustomed. In short, he has both his revenge—his work was generally recognized as being far superior to that of the former client who stiffed him—and he lives well.

Other Techniques

You can also become a columnist for a trade publication. You can frequent radio and television talk shows oriented to businesspeople. In short, use between 10 and 20 percent of your time on public relations and promotional activities. They may not generate huge contracts immediately, but they will eventually establish you as a leader in your field. As a leader, you may achieve the best situation of all: Clients will come to you and offer you freelance assignments.

Armed with the tools and techniques given in Part I, anyone who yearns to work as a freelance professional can feel confident that he or she can succeed. Most professionals already have the intelligence, the knowledge, and the skills to succeed on their own. Many who do not try simply believe that there is no room for them in their industry. This is almost always a false assumption. When I became a freelance writer, there were already more than 400,000 freelance writers competing to place work in 1,700 newspapers, 10,000 corporate publications, 1,200 book publishers, and several thousand magazines. But I believed that opportunity existed for me, and that my willingness to work—not my relatively average writing skills— would enable me to succeed. By my own and most other definitions of success for a freelance writer, I have done well, despite intense competition, a rapidly changing marketplace, and many obstacles. I do not believe that I am in any way unique. Just as you may not be unique in your industry or occupation. But, opportunity for you as a freelance professional does exist. You need only the willingness to try and the persistence to succeed despite the inevitable setbacks and challenges. And a little cash in the bank helps, too.

« PART II »

FREELANCER'S SOURCEBOOK

Part II lists business and trade associations, books, magazines, newsletters, magazine articles, and other sources of assistance for freelance professionals. These sources can help you start and succeed in your new career. They are divided into different categories of professional freelance work and apply to more than 100 individual occupations. By no means does this list cover all possible freelance occupations. The general references and source material can be used in any field. Listed first are the categories and a list of freelance careers. Use them to spur your thinking about your own field or help you make a choice of freelance careers.

Accounting, Finance and Tax Services

Accountant	Tax advisory service
Certified Public Accountant	Tax return preparation
Financial planner	Bookkeeping
Certified Financial Planner	Credit and collections investigator
Investment advisor	Collections and process server
Mortgage broker	

Advertising and Public Relations

Advertising copywriter

Consumer market researcher

Public relations copywriter

Public relations counselor

Advertising layout artist

Account executive

Art and Design

Commercial artist

Graphics designer

Stage designer

Paste-up and layout artist

Interior designer

Industrial designer

Package designer

Broadcasting

Radio disc jockey

Television personality

Radio and television announcer

Radio/television production engineer

Radio maintenance technician

Television broadcast technician

Business Teaching and Instruction

Seminar leader

Technical, vocational or trade school instructor

Part-time instructor at local college or community college

Adjunct professor at local college or university

Counseling and Education

Tutor children, adults and college students

Career and vocational counselor

Child guidance and development counselor

Human relations and marriage counselor

Psychologist or psychotherapist

Data Processing and Computers

Computer consultant

Systems analyst

Telecommunications or data
communications consultant

Microcomputer software
programmer

Microcomputer consultant

Software engineer

Minicomputer or mainframe software
programmer

Editorial Services

Freelance writer

Copy editor

Proofreader

Novelist

Speechwriter

Book reviewer

Promotion consultant

Book packager

Literary agent

Typesetter

Engineering and Scientific

Consulting engineer: aerospace, civil, surveying, mechanical, electrical, electronic, environmental, marine, hydraulic, etc.

Scientific researcher
Architect
Consulting chemist
Land and aerial surveyor
Environmental management
  consultant

Energy management consultant
Urban planner
House inspector
Construction engineer
Building remodeler/restorer

Exercise/Physical Fitness
Aerobics instructor
Swimming instructor
Sports instructor

Dance teacher
Karate and self-defense instructor

Exotics and Unusual
Skin diver
Private detective
Polygraph examiner
Tour/travel guide
Cruise host or hostess

Charter boat captain
Yacht broker
Image and fashion consultant
Genealogical researcher
Bartender

Legal Services
Court reporter
Paralegal researcher
Patent researcher
Private investigator

Insurance claim investigator
Insurance risk management consultant
Security service consultant
Anti-terrorist consultant

Medical and Health
Visiting nurse
Registered nurse
Licensed practical nurse
Nurses' aide
Midwife
Nutrition counselor
Childbirth education instructor

Home health aide
Physical therapist
Occupational therapist
Speech therapist
Masseur/masseuse
Laboratory technician

Personal Teaching
Music teacher
Art teacher
Photography instructor
Acting teacher

Cooking teacher
Personal skills instructor
Bridge, card game, gambling teacher

Photography and Video
Commercial and industrial
  photographer
Aerial photographer
Portrait photographer
Industrial film producer
Personal video services

Spot news photographer
Television news/video camera operator
Video editor
Video graphics designer
Photographer as artist

PROFESSIONAL, BUSINESS AND TRADE ASSOCIATIONS

General Consulting/Freelance Associations

American Association of Professional Consultants
912 Union Street
Manchester, NH 03104
(603) 623-5378

International Consultants Foundation
c/o Elinor Conversano
11612 Georgetown Court
Potomac, MD 20854
(301) 983-2709

Professional and Technical Consultants Association
1330 South Bascom Avenue
Suite D
San Jose, CA 95128

ACCOUNTING, FINANCE AND TAX ADVISORY SERVICES

American Accounting Association
5717 Bessie Drive
Sarasota, FL 33583
(813) 921-7747

American Association of Attorney-Certified Public Accountants
240001 Alicia Parkway
Suite 101
Mission Viejo, CA 92691
(714) 768-0336

American Association of Financial Professionals
P.O. Box 1928
Cocoa, FL 32923
(305) 632-8654

American Institute of Certified Public Accountants
(AICPA)
1211 Avenue of the Americas
New York, NY 10036
(212) 575-6200

American Society of Women Accountants
35 East Wacker Drive
Chicago, IL 60601
(312) 726-9030

Financial Accounting Foundation
P.O. Box 3821
High Ridge Park
Stamford, CT 06905
(203) 329-8401

Financial Analysts Federation
1633 Broadway
New York, NY 10019
(212) 957-2860

Foundation for Accounting Education
600 Third Avenue
New York, NY 10016
(212) 661-2020

Institute of Certified Financial Planners
3443 South Galena
Suite 190
Denver, CO 80231
(303) 751-7600

Institute of Certified Management Accountants
P.O. Box 405
Ten Paragon Drive
Montvale, NJ 07645
(201) 573-6300

Institute of Chartered Financial Analysts
P.O. Box 3668
Charlottesville, VA 22903
(804) 977-6600

Institute of Internal Auditors
249 Maitland Avenue
Altamonte Springs, FL 32701
(305) 830-7600

International Association for Financial Planning
Two Concourse Parkway
Suite 800
Atlanta, GA 30328
(404) 395-1605

International Association of Hospitality Accountants
Box 670
Keystone Heights, FL 32656
(904) 473-2744

National Association of Accountants
P.O. Box 433
Ten Paragon Drive
Montvale, NJ 07645
(201) 573-9000

National Association of Black Accountants
1010 Vermont Avenue, N.W.
Suite 901
Washington, DC 20005
(202) 783-7151

National Association of Estate Planning Councils
1010 Wisconsin Avenue, N.W.
Suite 630
Washington, DC 20007
(202) 965-7510

National Association of Personal Financial Advisors
3726 Olentangy River Road
Columbus, OH 43214
(614) 457-8200

National Conference of CPA Practitioners
330 West 58th Street
Suite 4C
New York, NY 10019
(212) 765-5255

National Society of Accountants for Cooperatives
Springfield Office Tower Building
Suite 802C
6320 Augusta Drive
Springfield, VA 22150

National Society of Public Accountants
1010 North Fairfield Street
Alexandria, VA 22314
(703) 549-6400

Society of Independent Financial Advisors
5954 South Monico Way
Englewood, CO 80111
(303) 850-9166

Credit and Collections Associations

American Collection Association
575 South 880 West
Orem, UT 84058

American Collectors Association
4040 West 70th Street
Minneapolis, MN 55435
(612) 926-6547

American Commercial Collectors Association
4040 West 70th Street
Minneapolis, MN 55435
(612) 925-0760

Credit Women International
6500 Chippewa
Suite 225
St. Louis, MO 63109
(314) 752-9535

National Association of Credit Management
National Institute of Credit
520 Eighth Avenue
New York, NY 10018
(212) 947-5070

Society of Certified Credit Executives
243 North Lindberg Boulevard
St. Louis, MO 63141
(314) 991-3030

Finance Associations

Financial Executives Institute
P.O. Box 1938
Ten Madison Avenue
Morristown, NJ 07690
(201) 898-4600

Foundation for Credit Education
P.O. Box 239
692 Brandywine Road
Nazareth, PA 18064
(215) 759-5367

National Association of Charitable Estate Counselors
P.O. Box 5359
Lake Worth, FL 33461
(305) 533-0880

National Corporate Cash Management Association
P.O. Box 7001
Newtown, CT 06470
(203) 426-3007

ADVERTISING AND PUBLIC RELATIONS

Advertising Council
825 Third Avenue
New York, NY 10022
(212) 758-0400

Advertising Research Foundation
3 East 54th Street
New York, NY 10022
(212) 751-5656

Advertising Women of New York
153 East 57th Street
New York, NY 10022
(212) 593-1950

American Advertising Federation (AAF)
1400 K Street, N.W.
Suite 1000
Washington, DC 20005
(202) 989-0089

American Association of Advertising Agencies (AAAA)
666 Third Avenue
13th Floor
New York, NY 10017
(212) 682-2500

Association of Fashion and Image Consultants
1133 15th Street, N.W.
Suite 620
Washington, DC 20005
(202) 293-5913

Association of National Advertisers
155 East 44th Street
New York, NY 10017
(212) 697-5950

Business/Professional Advertising Association
205 East 42nd Street
New York, NY 10017
(212) 661-0222

Institute of Personal Image Consultants
c/o Image Industry Publications
10 Bay Street Landing
Staten Island, NY 10301
(718) 273-3229

International Advertising Association
475 Fifth Avenue
New York, NY 10017
(212) 684-1583

Marketing Communications Executives International
c/o Grahame R. Hopkins
2602 McKinney Avenue
Dallas, TX 75204
(214) 871-1016

Marketing Research Association
111 East Wacker Drive
Suite 600
Chicago, IL 60601
(312) 644-6610

National Association of Co-Op Advertising Professionals
145 North Franklin Turnpike
Ramsey, NJ 07446
(201) 327-2667

Newspaper Advertising Bureau
1180 Avenue of the Americas
New York, NY 10036
(212) 921-5080

Public Relations Exchange
425 Lumber Exchange Building
Minneapolis, MN 55402
(612) 375-1190

Public Relations Society of America (PRSA)
845 Third Avenue
New York, NY 10022
(212) 826-1750

Radio Advertising Bureau
304 Park Avenue South
New York, NY 10010
(212) 254-4800

Retail Advertising Conference
67 East Oak Street
Chicago, IL 60611
(312) 280-9344

Specialty Advertising Association International
1404 Walnut Hill Lane
Irving, TX 75038
(214) 258-0404

Television Bureau of Advertising
477 Madison Avenue
New York, NY 10022
(212) 486-1111

Women in Advertising and Marketing
4200 Wisconsin Avenue
Suite 106-238
Washington, DC 20016
(301) 279-9093

Women Executives in Public Relations (WEPR)
P.O. Box 871
Murray Hill Station
New York, NY 10156
(212) 683-5438

ART AND DESIGN

American Artists Professional League
47 Fifth Avenue
New York, NY 10003
(212) 475-6650

American Color Print Society
c/o Bernard Kohn
8115 Cedar Road
Elkins Park, PA 19117
(215) 635-3115

American Portrait Society
P.O. Box 4168
Seal Beach, CA 90740
(213) 596-0139

American Society of Artists
P.O. Box 1326
Palatine, IL 60078
(312) 991-4748

American Watercolor Society
47 Fifth Avenue
New York, NY 10003
(212) 206-8986

Art Directors Club
250 Park Avenue South
New York, NY 10003
(212) 674-0500

Art Information Center
280 Broadway
Suite 412
New York, NY 10007
(212) 227-0282

Association of Editorial Cartoonists
c/o Ed Stein
Rocky Mountain News
400 West Colfax
Denver, CO 80204
(303) 892-5000

Caricaturists Society of America
218 West 47th Street
New York, NY 10036
(212) 221-2627

Cartoonists Guild
30 East 20th Street
New York, NY 10003
(212) 777-7353

Drawing Center
13 Greene Street
New York, NY 10012

National Academy of Design
1083 Fifth Avenue
New York, NY 10128
(212) 369-4880

National Art Museum of Sport
The University of New Haven
West Haven, CT 06516
(203) 932-7197

National Artists Equity Association
P.O. Box 28068
Central Station
Washington, DC 20038
(202) 628-9633

National Association of Women Artists
41 Union Square West
New York, NY 10003
(212) 675-1616

National Cartoonists Society
Nine Ebony Court
Brooklyn, NY 11229
(718) 743-6510

National League of American Pen Women
1300 17th Street, N.W.
Washington, DC 20036
(202) 785-1997

National Watercolor Society
c/o Arthur L. Kaye
5441 Alcove Avenue
North Hollywood, CA 91607

Package Designers Council
P.O. Box 3573
Grand Central Station
New York, NY 10017
(212) 682-1980

Pastel Society of America
15 Gramercy Park, South
New York, NY 10003
(212) 533-6931

Pen and Brush, Inc.
16 East 10th Street
New York, NY 10003
(212) 475-3669

The Print Club
1614 Latimer Street
Philadelphia, PA 19103
(215) 735-6090

Professional Picture Framers Association
4305 Sarellen Road
Richmond, VA 23231
(804) 226-0430

Silvermine Guild Center for the Arts
1037 Silvermine Road
New Canaan, CT 06840
(203) 966-5617

Society of Illustrators
128 East 63rd Street
New York, NY 10021
(212) 838-2560

Society of Motion Picture and Television Art Directors
14724 Ventura Boulevard
Penthouse Floor
Sherman Oaks, CA 91403
(818) 905-0599

Society of Photographers and Artists Representatives
1123 Broadway
Suite 914
New York, NY 10010
(212) 924-6023

Women's Caucus for Art
WCA National Office
Moore College of Art
20th, The Parkway
Philadelphia, PA 19103
(215) 854-0922

Graphic Arts Associations

Advertising Production Club of New York
545 West 45th Street
New York, NY 10036
(212) 245-6300

American Institute for Design and Drafting
966 Hungerford Drive
Suite 10-B
Rockville, MD 20854
(301) 294-8712

American Institute of Graphic Arts
1059 Third Avenue
New York, NY 10021
(212) 752-0813

American Institute of Technical Illustrators
2513 Forest Leaf Parkway
Suite 906
Ballwin, MO 63011
(314) 458-2248

Association of Graphic Arts Consultants
1730 North Lynn Street
Arlington, VA 22209
(703) 841-4811

Association of Professional Design Firms
117 North Jefferson Street
Suite 305
Chicago, IL 60606

Design International
3748 22nd Street
San Francisco, CA 94114
(415) 647-4700

Design Management Institute
621 Huntington Avenue
Boston, MA 02115
(617) 232-4496

Graphic Arts Technical Foundation
4615 Forbes Avenue
Pittsburgh, PA 15213
(412) 621-6941

Independent Signcrafters of America
P.O. Box 605
Marietta, OH 45750
(614) 374-3276

Institute for Graphic Communication
375 Commonwealth Avenue
Boston, MA 02115
(617) 267-9425

International Graphics, Inc.
c/o Stan Corfman
Marathon Oil Company
539 South Main Street
Findlay, OH 45840
(419) 422-2121

Printing Industries of America
1730 North Lynn Street
Arlington, VA 22209
(703) 841-8100

Proofreaders Club of New York
38-15 149th Street
Flushing, NY 11354
(718) 461-8509

Society of American Graphic Artists
32 Union Square
Room 1214
New York, NY 10003
(212) 260-5706

Society of Engineering Illustrators
c/o Ann O. Fletcher
Autodynamics Corp.
29380 Stephenson Highway
Madison Heights, MI 48071

Society of Environmental Graphics Designers
2200 Bridgeway Boulevard
Sausalito, CA 94965
(415) 332-3151

Society of Typographic Arts
233 East Ontario
Suite 301
Chicago, IL 60611
(312) 787-2018

Type Directors Club
545 West 45th Street
New York, NY 10036
(212) 245-6300

Women in Production
60 East 42nd Street
New York, NY 10165
(212) 682-8142

Interior Design Associations

American Society of Furniture Designers
P.O. Box 2688
High Point, NC 27261
(919) 884-4074

American Society of Interior Design
1430 Broadway
New York, NY 10018
(212) 944-9220

Decorators Club
c/o American Federation of Arts
41 East 65th Street
New York, NY 10021
(212) 998-7700

Institute of Business Designers
1155 Merchandise Mart
Chicago, IL 60654
(312) 467-1950

Interior Design Society
405 Merchandise Mart
Chicago, IL 60654
(312) 836-0777

International Association of Lighting Designers
18 East 16th Street
Suite 208
New York, NY 10003
(212) 206-1281

International Society of Interior Designers
8170 Beverly Boulevard
Suite 203
Los Angeles, CA 90048
(213) 655-2201

National Council for Interior Design Qualification
118 East 25th Street
New York, NY 10010
(212) 473-1188

National Council for Interior Horticultural Certification
115 Abbot Street
Andover, MA 01810
(617) 475-4433

Society of Certified Kitchen Designers
124 Main Street
Hackettstown, NJ 07840
(201) 852-0033

BROADCASTING AND FILM

Academy of Science Fiction, Fantasy and Horror Films
334 West 54th Street
Los Angeles, CA 90037
(213) 752-5811

American Film Institute
John F. Kennedy Center for the Performing Arts
Washington, DC 20566
(202) 828-4000

Association of Independent Commercial Producers
100 East 42nd Street
16th Floor
New York, NY 10017
(212) 867-5720

Association of Independent Video and Filmmakers
625 Broadway
9th Floor
New York, NY 10012
(212) 473-3400

Black American Cinema Society
3617 Monclair Street
Los Angeles, CA 90018
(213) 737-3292

Black Filmmaker Foundation
80 Eighth Avenue
Suite 1704
New York, NY 10011
(212) 924-1198

Children's Film and Television Center of America
School of Cinema/Television
University of Southern California
Los Angeles, CA 90089
(213) 743-8632

Children's Television Workshop
One Lincoln Plaza
New York, NY 10023
(212) 595-3456

Independent Feature Project
21 West 86th Street
New York, NY 10024
(212) 496-0909

International Animated Film Society
5301 Laurel Canyon Boulevard
Suite 250
North Hollywood, CA 91607
(818) 508-5224

International Association of Independent Producers
P.O. Box 2801
Washington, DC 20013
(202) 638-5595

International Documentary Association
8489 West Third Street
Los Angeles, CA 90048
(213) 655-7089

Music Video Association
P.O. Box 1606
Beltsville, MD 20705

Women in Film
8489 West Third Street
Suite 85
Los Angeles, CA 90048
(213) 651-3680

BUSINESS SERVICES AND INSTRUCTION

American Management Association
135 West 50th Street
New York, NY 10020
(212) 586-8100

American Society of Pension Actuaries
1413 K Street
Fifth Floor
Washington, DC 20005
(202) 737-4360

The Association of Management Consulting Firms
230 Park Avenue
New York, NY 10169
(212) 697-9693

Association of Management Consultants
500 North Michigan Avenue
Chicago, IL 60611
(312) 266-1261

Association of Part-Time Professionals
Flow General Building
7655 Old Springhouse Road
McLean, VA 22102
(703) 734-7975

Association of Productivity Specialists
200 Park Avenue
Suite 303E
New York, NY 10016

Council of Communication Management
P.O. Box 3970
Grand Central Station
New York, NY 10163

Employee Relocation Council
1720 N Street, N.W.
Washington, DC 20036
(202) 857-0857

Industrial Relations Counselors
P.O. Box 1530
New York, NY 10101
(212) 541-6086

Institute of Certified Professional Managers
208B Harrison Hall
James Madison University
Harrisonburg, VA 22807
(703) 568-6909

Institute of Management Consultants
19 West 44th Street
Suite 810
New York, NY 10036
(212) 921-2885

International Society of Certified Employee Benefit Specialists
18700 West Bluemound Road
Brookfield, WI 53005
(414) 786-8771

National Association of Pension Consultants and Administrators
c/o John W. Baker
P.O. Box 53017
359 East Paces Ferry Road, N.E.
Atlanta, GA 30355
(404) 231-0100

Society of Professional Management Consultants
163 Engle Street
Englewood, NJ 07631
(201) 569-6668

Women in Management
P.O. Box 11268
Chicago, IL 60611
(312) 963-0134

DATA PROCESSING AND COMPUTERS

American Association of Computer Professionals
72 Valley Hill Road
Stockbridge, GA 30281
(404) 474-7874

American Electronics Association
P.O. Box 10045
2670 Hanover Street
Palo Alto, CA 94303
(415) 857-9300

American Federation of Information Processing
1899 Preston White Drive
Reston, VA 22091
(703) 620-8900

Association of Computer Professionals
230 Park Avenue
New York, NY 10169
(212) 599-3019

Association of Data Processing Service Organizations
1300 North 17th Street
Suite 300
Arlington, VA 22209

Association of Electronic Cottagers
P.O. Box 604
Sierra Madre, CA 91024
(818) 355-0800

Association of Information Systems Professionals
1015 North York Road
Willow Grove, PA 19090
(215) 657-6300

Association of the Institute for Certification of Data Processing
    Professionals
2200 East Devon Avenue
Des Plaines, IL 60018

Association for Women in Computing
407 Hillmoor Drive
Silver Spring, MD 20901

Black Data Processing Associates
P.O. Box 2254
Philadelphia, PA 19103

Data Processing Management Association
505 Busse Highway
Park Ridge, IL 60068
(312) 825-8124

EDP Auditors Association
373 South Schmale Road
Carol Stream, IL 60187
(312) 682-1200

Electronic Industries Association
2001 Eye Street, N.W.
Washington, DC 20006
(202) 457-4900

Electronics Technicians Association
825 East Franklin Street
Greencastle, IN 46135
(317) 653-3849

Independent Computer Consultants Association
P.O. Box 27412
St. Louis, MO 63141
(314) 997-4633

International Organization of Women in Telecommunications
c/o Anne Bailey
2308 Oakwood Lane
Arlington, TX 76012
(817) 275-0683

International Society of Certified Electronics Technicians
2708 West Berry
Suite #8
Fort Worth, TX 76109
(817) 921-9101

National Computer Graphics Association
2722 Merrilee Drive
Suite 200
Fairfax, VA 22031
(703) 698-9600

North American Computer Service Association
506 Georgetown Drive
Casselberry, FL 32707
(305) 331-0181

Office Automation Society International
15269 Mimosa Trail
Dumfries, VA 22026
(703) 690-3880

Semiconductor Equipment and Material Institute
625 Willis Street
Suite 212
Mountain View, CA 94043
(415) 964-5111

Semiconductor Industry Association
805 East Middlefield Road
San Jose, CA 95129
(408) 246-1181

Society of Office Automation Professionals
AMS Building
2360 Maryland Road
Willow Grove, PA 19090
(215) 659-4300

Society of Telecommunications Consultants
One Rockefeller Plaza
Suite 1410
New York, NY 10020
(212) 582-3909

Women in Data Processing
P.O. Box 880866
San Diego, CA 92108
(619) 569-5615

Women in Information Processing
Lock Box 39173
Washington, DC 20016
(202) 328-6161

EDITORIAL SERVICES

American News Women's Club
1607 22nd Street, N.W.
Washington, DC 20008
(202) 332-6770

American Society of Business Press Editors
4196 Porter Road
North Olmstead, OH 44070
(216) 734-9522

American Society of Journalists & Authors
1501 Broadway
Suite 1907
New York, NY 10036
(212) 997-0947

American Society of Magazine Editors
575 Lexington Avenue
New York, NY 10022
(212) 752-0055

Association of Professional Writing Consultants
3924 South Troost
Tulsa, OK 74105
(918) 743-4793

Associated Writing Programs
Old Dominion University
Norfolk, VA 23508
(804) 440-3839

Authors Guild
234 West 44th Street
New York, NY 10036
(212) 398-0838

The Author's League of America, Inc.
234 West 44th Street
New York, NY 10036
(212) 39-9198

Aviation/Space Writers Association
1000 Connecticut Avenue, N.W.
Suite 707
Washington, DC 20036
(202) 296-4394

Bread Loaf Writers Conference
Middlebury College
Middlebury, VT 05753
(802) 388-3711

Committee of Small Magazine Editors and Publishers
P.O. Box 703
San Francisco, CA 94101
(415) 922-9490

Computer Press Association
P.O. Box 1506
Homewood, IL 60430
(312) 798-6496

Council of Writers Organizations
1501 Broadway
Suite 1907
New York, NY 10036
(212) 997-0947

Editorial Freelancers Association
20 East 20th Street
Room 305
New York, NY 10011
(212) 677-3357

Feminist Writer's Guild
P.O. Box 14055
Chicago, IL 60614
(312) 929-1326

Freelance Network
P.O. Box 767
Sierra Madre, CA 91024
(213) 655-4476

International Association of Business Communicators
870 Market Street
Suite 940
San Francisco, CA 94102
(415) 433-3400

International Black Writers
P.O. Box 1030
Chicago, IL 60690
(312) 995-5195

International Labor Communications Association
815 16th Street, N.W.
Washington, DC 20006
(202) 637-5068

International Women's Writing Guild
P.O. Box 810
Gracie Station
New York, NY 10028
(212) 737-7536

Mystery Writers of America
150 Fifth Avenue
New York, NY 10011
(212) 255-7005

National Association of Media Women
1185 Niskey Lake Road, S.W.
Atlanta, GA 30331
(404) 344-5862

National Association of Science Writers
P.O. Box 294
Greenlawn, NY 11740
(516) 757-5664

The National Writers Club, Inc.
1450 South Havan
Suite 620
Aurora, CO 80012
(303) 751-7844

National Writers Union
13 Astor Place
New York, NY 10003
(212) 254-0279

New York Business Press Editors
P.O. Box 5771
Grand Central Station
New York, NY 10017
(212) 683-9294

New York Financial Writers' Association
P.O. Box 21
Syosset, NY 11791
(516) 921-7766

Newspaper Food Editors and Writers Association
c/o Jane Baker
The Phoenix Gazette
120 East Van Buren
Phoenix, AZ 85001
(602) 271-8948

Romance Writers of America
5206 FM 1960
Suite 207
Houston, TX 77069
(713) 440-6885

Science Fiction Writers of America
P.O. Box H
Wharton, NJ 07885

Small Press Writers and Artists Organization
c/o Audrey Parente
411 Main Trail
Ormond Beach, FL 32074

Society of Publication Designers
25 West 43rd Street
New York, NY 10036
(212) 354-8585

Society for Technical Communication
815 15th Street, N.W.
Suite 506
Washington, DC 20005
(202) 737-0035

Western Writers of America
1753 Victoria
Sheridan, WY 82801
(307) 672-2079

Women in Communications
National Headquarters
P.O. Box 9561
Austin, TX 78766
(512) 346-9875

ENGINEERING AND SCIENTIFIC

Acoustical Society of America
335 East 45th Street
New York, NY 10017

Aerospace Industries Association of America
1725 DeSales Street, N.W.
Washington, DC 20036
(202) 429-4600

Alliance of Women in Architecture
P.O. Box 5136
F.D.R. Station
New York, NY 10022
(212) 744-5200

American Academy of Environmental Engineers
P.O. Box 269
93 Main Street
Annapolis, MD 21404
(301) 267-9377

American Association of Cost Engineers
308 Monongahela Building
Morgantown, WV 26505
(304) 296-8444

American Chemical Society
1155 16th Street, N.W.
Washington, DC 20036
(202) 872-4600

American Geophysical Union
2000 Florida Avenue, N.W.
Washington, DC 20009
(202) 462-6903

American Institute of Aeronautics and Astronautics
1633 Broadway
New York, NY 10036
(212) 581-4300

American Institute of Architects
1735 New York Avenue, N.W.
Washington, DC 20006
(202) 626-7300

American Institute of Building Design
1412 19th Street
Sacramento, CA 95814
(916) 447-2422

American Institute of Chemical Engineers
345 East 47th Street
New York, NY 10017
(212) 705-7338

American Institute of Chemists
7315 Wisconsin Avenue, N.W.
Bethesda, MD 20814
(301) 652-2447

American Institute of Professional Geologists
7828 Vance Drive
Suite 103
Arvada, CO 80003
(303) 431-0831

American Institute of Plant Engineers
3975 Erie Avenue
Cincinnati, OH 45208
(513) 561-6000

American Society for Metals
Metals Park, OH 44073
(216) 338-5151

American Society of Agricultural Engineers
2950 Niles Road
St. Joseph, MI 49085
(616) 429-0300

American Society of Certified Engineering Technicians
P.O. Box 7789
Shawnee Mission, KS 66207
(913) 451-4938

American Society of Civil Engineers
345 East 47th Street
New York, NY 10017
(212) 705-7496

American Society of Heating, Refrigerating and Air-Conditioning
    Engineers
1791 Tullie Circle, N.E.
Atlanta, GA 30329
(404) 636-8400

American Society of Home Inspectors
1010 Wisconsin Avenue, N.W.
Suite 630
Washington, DC 20007
(202) 842-3096

American Society of Inventors
P.O. Box 58426
Philadelphia, PA 19102
(215) 546-6601

American Society of Mechanical Engineers
345 East 47th Street
New York, NY 10017
(212) 705-7722

American Society of Naval Engineers
1452 Duke Street
Alexandria, VA 22314
(703) 836-6727

American Society of Plumbing Engineers
3617 Thousand Oaks Boulevard
Suite 210
Westlake, CA 91362

American Society of Professional Estimators
6911 Richmond Highway
Suite 230
Alexandria, VA 22306
(703) 765-2700

Association for Computing Machinery
11 West 42nd Street
New York, NY 10036
(212) 869-7440

Association of Consulting Chemists and Chemical Engineers
50 East 41st Street
Suite 92
New York, NY 10017

Association of Energy Engineers
4025 Pleasantdale Road
Suite 340
Atlanta, GA 30340
(404) 447-5083

Chemical Industry for Minorities in Engineering
P.O. Box 2558
Midland, MI 48640
(517) 636-3454

Council of Biology Editors
9650 Rockville Pike
Bethesda, MD 20814
(301) 530-7036

Electrochemical Society
Ten South Main Street
Pennington, NJ 08534
(609) 737-1902

Industrial Designers Society of America
1360 Beverly Road
McLean, VA 22101
(703) 556-0919

Institute of Electrical and Electronics Engineers
345 East 47th Street
New York, NY 10017
(212) 705-7900

Institute of Industrial Engineers
25 Technology Park/Atlanta
Norcross, GA 30092
(404) 449-0460

Materials Research Society
9800 McKnight Road
Suite 327
Pittsburgh, PA 15237
(412) 367-3003

National Institute for Certification in Engineering Technologies
1420 King Street
Alexandria, VA 22314
(703) 684-2835

National Society of Architectural Engineers
P.O. Box 395
Lawrence, KS 66044
(913) 864-3434

National Society of Black Engineers
1101 Connecticut Avenue, N.W.
Suite 700
Washington, DC 20036
(212) 857-1100

National Society of Professional Engineers
1420 King Street
Alexandria, VA 22314
(703) 684-2800

Society of American Registered Architects
320 North Michigan Avenue
Chicago, IL 60601
(312) 263-3311

Society of Biomedical Equipment Technicians
1901 North Fort Meyer Drive
Suite 602
Arlington, VA 22209
(703) 525-4890

Society of Flight Test Engineers
P.O. Box 4047
Lancaster, CA 93539
(805) 948-3067

Society of Hispanic Professional Engineers
5400 East Olympiad Boulevard
Suite 120
Los Angeles, CA 90022
(213) 725-3970

Society of Independent Professional Earth Scientists
4925 Greenville Avenue
Suite 170
Dallas, TX 75206
(214) 363-1780

Society of Logistics Engineers
303 Williams Avenue
Suite 922
Huntsville, AL 35801
(205) 539-3800

Society of Manufacturing Engineers
P.O. Box 930
One SME Drive
Dearborn, MI 48121
(313) 271-1500

Society for Marketing Professional Services
801 North Fairfax Street
Suite 215
Alexandria, VA 22314
(703) 549-6117

Society of Motion Picture and Television Engineers
595 West Hartsdale Avenue
White Plains, NY 10607
(914) 472-6606

Society of Naval Architects and Marine Engineers
One World Trade Center
Suite 1369
New York, NY 10048
(212) 432-0310

Society of Plastics Engineers
14 Fairfield Drive
Brookfield Center, CT 06805
(203) 775-0471

Society of Women Engineers
345 East 47th Street
Room 305
New York, NY 10017
(212) 705-7855

SPIE—The International Society for Optical Engineering
P.O. Box 10
1022 19th Street
Bellingham, WA 98227
(206) 676-3290

Technical Marketing Society of America
3711 Long Beach Boulevard
Suite 609
Long Beach, CA 90807
(213) 595-0254

EXOTICS AND UNUSUAL

American Institute of Floral Designers
113 West Franklin Street
Baltimore, MD 21201
(301) 752-3318

American Association of Credit Counselors
P.O. Box 372
Grayslake, IL 60030
(312) 223-0355

American Association of Professional Bridal Consultants
Association of Bridal Consultants
200 Chestnutland Road
New Milford, CT 06776
(203) 355-0464

American Bartenders Association
P.O. Box 11447
Bradenton, FL 34282

American Society of Interpreters
P.O. Box 5558
Washington, DC 22016
(301) 657-3337

American Translators Association
109 Croton Avenue
Ossining, NY 10562
(914) 941-1500

Council of International Investigators
P.O. Box 5609
Baltimore, MD 21210
(301) 323-4480

Foodservice Consultants Society International
12345 30th Avenue, N.E.
Suite H
Seattle, WA 98125
(206) 367-7274

Freelance Finders Network
P.O. Box 1456
Stillwater, OK 74076
(405) 624-9994

International Association of Computer Crime Investigators
c/o Jack Bologna, President
150 North Main Street
Plymouth, MI 48170
(313) 459-8787

National Association of Flight Instructors
Ohio State University Airport
P.O. Box 793
Dublin, OH 43017
(614) 889-6148

National Association of Investigative Specialists
8200 Cameron
Building D, Suite 100-B
Austin, TX 78753
(512) 832-0355

National Auctioneers Association
8880 Ballentine
Overland Park, KS 66214
(913) 541-8084

Stuntmen's Association of Motion Pictures
4810 Whitsett Avenue
North Hollywood, CA 91607
(818) 766-4334

Stunt Women of America
202 Vance
Pacific Palisades, CA 90272
(213) 454-8228

World Association of Detectives
P.O. Box 3674
Cincinnati, OH 45326
(513) 891-2002

PHOTOGRAPHY AND VIDEO

Advertising Photographers of America
175 Fifth Avenue
New York, NY 10010

American Photographic Artisans Guild
637 South Shore Drive
Madison, WI 53715
(608) 255-5787

American Society of Magazine Photographers
205 Lexington Avenue
New York, NY 10016
(212) 889-9144

American Society of Photographers
P.O. Box 52900
Tulsa, OK 74152
(918) 743-2122

American Society of Picture Professionals
P.O. Box 5283
Grand Central Station
New York, NY 10063
(212) 685-3870

Associated Photographers International
P.O. Box 4055
22231 Mulholland Highway
Suite 119
Woodland Hills, CA 91365
(818) 888-9270

Evidence Photographers International Council
701 Wyoming Avenue
Scranton, PA 18509
(717) 344-2299

International Fire Photographers Association
P.O. Box 201
Elmhurst, IL 60216
(312) 530-3097

National Freelance Photographers Association
10 South Pine Street
Doylestown, PA 18901
(215) 348-5578

National Press Photographers Association
P.O. Box 1146
Durham, NC 27702
(919) 489-3700

Photographic Society of America
2005 Walnut Street
Philadelphia, PA 19103
(215) 563-1663

Professional Photographers of America
1090 Executive Way
Des Plaines, IL 60018
(312) 299-8161

Professional Women Photographers
c/o Photographics Unlimited
43 West 22nd Street, 11th Floor
New York, NY 10010
(212) 255-9676

Wedding Photographers International
P.O. Box 2003
1312 Lincoln Boulevard
Santa Monica, CA 90406
(213) 451-0090

BIBLIOGRAPHY

This section is divided both by types of books and type of free-lance career. Many of the listings are "how-to," that is, they help freelance professionals succeed in starting and managing their own business. Applicable magazine articles are listed at the end of each occupational section.

≪ BUSINESS AND MANAGEMENT CONSULTING PRACTICE ≫

Books

————, *The Consultant's Kit: Operating Your Own Successful Consulting Business*, Denver, CO: Gordon Printing, 1987.

Albert, Kenneth J., *How to Solve Business Problems: The Consultant's Approach to Business Problem Solving*, New York: McGraw-Hill, 1983.

Bermont, Hubert, *The Complete Consultant: A Roadmap to Success*, The Consultants Library, Washington, D.C.: Bermont Books, 1982.

Cohen, William A., *How to Make It Big as a Consultant*, New York: American Management Association, 1985.

Gray, Douglas, *Start & Run a Profitable Consulting Business: A Step-By-Step Business Plan*, Seattle, WA: ISC Press, 1984.

Greenfield, W.M., *Successful Management Consulting*, Englewood Cliffs, N.J.: Prentice-Hall, 1987.

Greiner, Larry E. and Metzger, Robert O., *Consulting to Management*, Englewood Cliffs, N.J.: Prentice-Hall, 1983.

Holtz, Herman, *The Consultant's Edge: Using the Computer as a Marketing Tool*, New York: John Wiley & Sons, 1985.

————, *The Consultant's Guide to Proposal Writing: How to Satisfy Your Clients and Double Your Income*, New York: John Wiley & Sons, 1986.

————, *How to Become a More Successful Consultant with Your Personal Computer*, The Consultant's Library, Washington, D.C.: Bermont Books, 1985.

Holtz, Herman, *How to Succeed as an Independent Consultant*, New York: John Wiley & Sons, 1983.

Johnson, Barbara, *Private Consulting: How to Turn Experience into Employment Dollars*, Englewood Cliffs, N.J.: Prentice-Hall, 1982.

Kelley, Robert E., *CONSULTING: The Complete Guide to a Profitable Career*, New York: Charles Scribner's Sons, 1986.

Kennedy, James H., ed., *Public Relations for Management Consultants*, Fitzwilliam, N.H.: *Consultants News*, 1980.

Kishel, Gregory F. & Kishel, Patricia G., *Cashing in on the Consulting Boom*, New York: John Wiley & Sons, 1985.

Lant, Jeffrey, "The Consultant's Kit: Establishing & Operating Your Successful Consulting Business," 2nd Ed., Enterprise Series, vol. 1, *JLA Publications*, 1985.

————, "Tricks of the Trade: The Complete Guide to Succeeding in the Advice Business," Enterprise Series, vol. 4, *JLA Publications*, 1986.

Marcus, Bruce W., *Competing for Clients: The Complete Guide to Marketing and Promoting Professional Services*, New York: Pathfinder Press, 1985.

Schneider, Richard, *The Management of Management Consulting Firms*, New York: Irvington Press, 1987.

Shenson, Howard L., *How to Strategically Negotiate the Consulting Contract*, Washington, D.C.: Bermont Books, 1980.

————, *The Successful Consultant's Guide to Fee Setting*, Washington, D.C.: Bermont Books, 1980.

Stryker, Steven C., *Guide to Successful Consulting with Forms, Letters and Checklists*, Englewood Cliffs, N.J.: Prentice-Hall, 1984.

————, *Principles & Practices of Professional Consulting*, The Consultant's Library, Washington, D.C.: Bermont Books, 1982.

Tepper, Ron, *Become a Top Consultant: How the Experts Do It*, New York: John Wiley & Sons, 1987.

————, *The Consultant's Problem Solver*, New York: John Wiley & Sons, 1987.

Weinberg, Gerald M., *The Secrets of Consulting: Guide to Giving and Getting Advice*, New York: Dorset House Publishing, 1985.

Magazine Articles

Changing Times, "Getting Paid for Giving Advice," vol. 39, August, 1985, p. 59.

Financial World, "It Pays to Specialize," vol. 154, August 21, 1985, p. 15.

Journal of Business Strategy, "New Trends in Strategic Consulting Industry," vol. 7, Summer, 1986, pp. 43–55.

The Office, "The Client and the Consultant: A Perspective," vol. 103, April, 1986, p. 128.

Sloan Management Review, "Growth Strategies for Consulting in the Next Decade," vol. 27, Winter, 1986, p. 61.

Training, "How to Contract for Speaker Insurance—Before the Meeting," vol. 23, July, 1986, page 13.

≪ ADVERTISING ≫

These books and publications help the freelance professional make better use of his or her advertising dollars.

Bellavance, Diane, *Advertising & Public Relations for a Small Business*, 3rd Edition, Boston, MA: DBA Books, 1985.

Brannen, William H., *Advertising and Sales Promotion, Cost Effective Techniques for Your Small Business*, Englewood Cliffs, N.J.: Prentice-Hall, 1983.

Braun, Irwin, *Building a Successful Professional Practice with Advertising*, Ann Arbor: Books on Demand, University of Michigan, 1981.

David, Bruce E., *A Shoestring Approach to Profitable Advertising: A Handbook for Small Business*, 4th ed., Tucson, AZ: EJP Publishing Company, 1987.

Gray, Ernest A., *Profitable Methods for Small Business Advertising*, Small Business Management Series, New York: John Wiley & Sons, 1984.

King, Norman, *Big Sales from Small Spaces: Tips & Techniques for Effective Small Space Advertising*, New York: Facts on File, 1986.

Ross, Stewart H., *The Management of Business-to-Business Advertising: A Working Guide for Small to Mid-Size Companies*, Westport, CT: Greenwood Press, 1986.

Rush, Paul, *Selling with Video*, White Plains, NY: Knowledge Industry Publications, 1987.

Slutsky, Jeff, and Woodruff, Woddy, *Streetfighting: Low-Cost Advertising-Promotion Strategies for Your Small Business*, Englewood Cliffs, N.J.: Prentice-Hall, 1983.

Wagner, W.F., *Advertising in the Yellow Pages: How To Boost Profits and Avoid Pitfalls*, Baltimore, MD: Heritage Press, 1986.

Walker, Morton, *How to Advertise and Promote Your Professional Practice*, New York: Macmillan, 1982.

Advertising-Direct Mail

Books

Holtz, H., *Mail Order Magic: Sure-Fire Techniques to Expand Any Business By Direct Mail*, New York: McGraw-Hill, 1983.

Premier Publishers, Inc., *How to Prepare Your Own Mail Order Catalog (Without Merchandise & For Pennies)*, Houston: Premier Publishers, 1986.

Sackheim, Maxwell, *How to Advertise Yourself*, New York: Free Press, 1978.

Stilson, Galen, *How to Write & Design Money-Making Response Advertisements*, Mail Order Success Series No. 3, Houston: Premier Publishers, 1984.

————, *The Success of How-To's of Money-Making Direct Mail*, Mail Order Success Series, No. 4, Houston: Premier Publishers, 1985.

Throckmorton, Joan, *Winning Direct Response Advertising: How to Recognize It, Evaluate It, Inspire It & Create It*, Englewood Cliffs, N.J.: Prentice-Hall, 1986.

Magazine Articles

Across the Board, "How to Sell Almost Anything by Direct Mail," vol. 23, November, 1986, p. 45.

American Demographics, "Periodontists' Mail Order Smiles," vol. 9, February, 1987, p. 20.

American Printer, "Business Cards Are an Important Promotional Vehicle That Should Not Be Overlooked," vol. 194, June, 1985, p. 100.

———, "Need a Promotion Campaign That Really Packs a Punch? Follow the Three I's—Information Plus Individuality and Innovation," vol. 198, December, 1986, p. 102.

Bank Marketing, "Put the Stamp on Direct Mail with These 14 Steps," vol. 19, June, 1987, p. 22.

Building Design and Construction, "Nine Steps to Successful Direct Mail Marketing," vol. 27, September, 1986, p. 46.

Direct Marketing, "Coordinating Direct Marketing with a Field Sales Force," vol. 49, June, 1986, p. 54.

———, "Keeping Letters Alive," vol. 49, April, 1987, p. 68.

———, "More Self-Evident Truths," five-part series on writing effective direct mail copy, vol. 48, November, 1986, vol. 49, March, 1987.

———, "Persuade Business Prospects to Buy by Mail," vol. 50, May, 1987, p. 106.

———, "The Brochure," four-part series, vol. 50, February–May, 1987.

Management Today, "When Being Direct Pays Dividends," November, 1985, p. 49.

The Professional Report, "How to Build Sales and Profits by Developing Your Mailing List," vol. 15, November, 1985, p. 19.

———, "How to Get Better Results from Your Business-to-Business Mailings," vol. 14, December, 1984, p. 23.

Sales & Marketing Management, "Direct Mail, Bibliography," vol. 134, Jan. 14, 1985, p. 61.

Advertising Publications for Freelance Professionals

Bly, Robert W., *The Copywriter's Handbook,* New York: Dodd, Mead, 1985.

Crawford, Tad and Kopelman, Arie, *Selling Your Graphic Design and Illustration: The Complete Marketing, Business and Legal Guide,* New York: St. Martin's Press, 1981.

Fulton, Sue and Buxton, Edward, *Advertising Freelancers,* New York: Executive Communications, 1985.

Gold, Ed, *The Business of Graphic Design,* New York: Watson-Guptill, 1985.

Gross, Len and Stirling, John T., *How to Build a Small Advertising Agency and Run It at a Profit,* Alameda, CA: Kentwood Publications, 1984.

Kopelman, Arie and Crawford, Tad, *Selling Your Photography: The Complete Marketing, Business and Legal Guide,* New York: St. Martin's Press, 1980.

Lockett, David, *Getting New Business Leads: A Guide for Advertising Agencies,* Chicago, IL: National Textbook Co., 1981.

Morgan, Jim, *Marketing for the Small Design Firm,* New York: Watson-Guptill, 1984.

Rotman, Morris B., *Opportunities in Public Relations,* Chicago, IL: National Textbook Co., 1983.

Advertising How-To Audio Cassettes

Gross, Len, *How to Build a Small Agency,* Alameda, CA: Kentwood Publications, 1985.

Stirling, John, *Make Your Small Agency Turn a Profit,* Alameda, CA: Kentwood Publications, 1985.

≪ ARCHITECTS ≫

Architectural Record, "Brochures Are Serious Business," vol. 174, September, 1986, p. 45.

Progressive Architect, "Strategies for the Small Firm," vol. 68, April, 1987, p. 67.

≪ ARTS ≫

Graphics Arts Monthly, "Reflections of a Consultant," vol. 57, October, 1985, p. 202.

≪ COMPUTERS AND DATA PROCESSING ≫

Books

Roetzheim, William H., *Proposal Writing for the DP Consultant,* Englewood Cliffs, N.J.: Prentice-Hall, 1986.

Tomczak, Steven P., *Successful Consulting for Engineers and Data Processing Professionals,* New York: John Wiley & Sons, 1982.

Magazine Articles

Computer Decisions, "Advise and Consult," vol. 18, Oct. 28, 1986, p. 11.

———, "The Tides Turn for Micro Consultants," vol. 18, April 22, 1986, p. 58.

Computerworld, "A Day in the Life of a Consultant," vol. 19, Sept. 21, 1986, p. 21.

———, "Choosing and Using Computer Consultants," vol. 19, Sept. 2, 1985, p. 42.

———, "The Secrets of Consulting," vol. 20, Feb. 17, 1986, p. 57.

Data Management, "Effective Consultant-Client Interaction Requires Teamwork," vol. 25, July, 1987, p. 23.

———, "Effective Use of DP Consultants Requires Communications," vol. 25., February, 1987, p. 28.

———, "DPMA Surveys Fallout From 1706: IRS Tries to Clarify the Tax Issue," vol. 25, July, 1987, p. 7.

Datamation, "Going It Alone," Reader's Forum, vol. 30, September 1, 1984, p. 207.

———, "Is Anyone Really Using Computer Consultants?" vol. 32, Oct. 15, 1986, p. 99.

———, "Repeal Section 1706: How Should Contractors Be Taxed?" vol. 33, June 1, 1987, p. 90.

InfoSystems, "Consultants: The Corporate Cure-All?" vol. 33, July, 1986, p. 38.

Personnel Administrator, "The Systems Consultant: Friend or Foe," vol. 32, March, 1987, p. 30.

The Professional Report, "How to Find and Work with a Computer Consultant," vol. 15, August, 1985, p. 16.

≪ Consulting Engineers ≫

This listing provides general and specific books and magazine articles for all engineering freelance professionals, from aerospace to petroleum.

Books

American Consulting Engineers Council, *ACEC Membership Directory,* 1986–1987, Washington, D.C.: ACEC, 1986.

———, *Consulting Engineering Practice Manual,* New York: McGraw-Hill, 1981.

———, *Public Relations Guide for Consulting Engineers,* Washington, D.C.: ACEC, 1982.

Kaye, Harvey, *Inside the Technical Consulting Business: Launching & Building Your Independent Practice,* New York: John Wiley & Sons, 1986.

Kirby, Jonell H., *Consultation: Practice & Practitioner,* Muncie, IN: Accelerated Development, 1985.

Society of Automotive Engineers, *Automotive Consultants Directory,* Detroit, MI: SAE, 1986.

Magazine Articles

General

Control Engineering, "Trends in Control: More Consultants Available, But Need Directory," vol. 31, Dec., 1984, p. 144.

Energy User News, "American Consulting Engineers Council May Lower Contractor Insurance Costs," vol. 11, Oct. 27, 1986, p. 19.

Machine Design, "Do-It-Yourself Career Planning," vol. 57, March 21, 1985, p. 107.

———, "How to Become a Business-Savvy Engineer," vol. 58, Feb. 6, 1986, p. 91.

———, "The Politics of Selling Ideas: The Power of Persuasion Can Increase Your Effectiveness," vol. 57, Nov. 7, 1985, p. 97.

New Orleans/Louisiana Business, "ASCE (American Society of Civil Engineers) Sets Directives in Professional Responsibility and Public Safety," vol. 20, Sept., 1986, p. 8LBP.

Pulp & Paper, "Career-Planning Programs Help Engineers Map Long-Term Goals," vol. 59, Sept., 1985, p. 94.

Aeronautical/Aerospace Engineers

Electronic News, "Mergers, Project Cuts Displace Some Engineers, Demand Brisk for Select Skills," vol. 32, Oct. 20, 1986, p. 48.

Automobile / Automotive Engineers

Automotive Industries, "Revolution by Design: Detroit's New Guns for Hire—You Say You Want a Revolution? How About $1 Billion in Outside Automotive Design by 1990?" vol. 167, March, 1987, p. 34.

Automotive News, "Designing by Contract: Outside Firms Can Still Do It Quicker and Cheaper Than the Big Three," May 19, 1986, p. D12.

Crain's Detroit Business, "Auto Engineering Firms Grow Rapidly, Diversify," vol. 2, March 3, 1986, p. 1.

Ward's Auto World, "'Tradeoff Has Been More Than Fair,' Giving Up Big 3 Perks for Other Rewards," vol. 23, March, 1987, p. 69.

Chemical Engineers

Chemical & Engineering News, "Career Planning," (information sources and directory), vol. 64, Oct. 27, 1986, p. 58.

Plastics World, "Profile of the Research & Development Professional," vol. 44, April, 1986, p. 37.

————, "Profile of the Design Engineering Professional," vol. 44, April, 1986, p. 39.

Petroleum Engineers

New York Times, "From Oil Industry to Teaching Science," vol. 136, Oct. 21, 1986, p. 21.

Transportation Engineers

Mass Transit, "Consultants Guide," (Directory), vol. 13, August, 1986, p. 14.

Women in Engineering

Business Journal of San Jose, CA, "Despite Gains, Women Engineers Seek Parity," vol. 4, Oct. 27, 1986, p. 1.

Computerworld, "Women in Computer Services," vol. 18, Nov. 12, 1984, p. O41.

Data Communications, "A Female Engineer Makes Connections for Others in the Field," vol. 14, May, 1985, p. 101.

EDN, "Women in Engineering Serve as Role Models to Fight Image of Male-Dominated Profession," vol. 31, May 15, 1986, p. 271.

New York Times, "Optimism on Women Engineers," vol. 136, July 21, 1987, p. D17.

Technology Review, "Will Women Make a Difference," vol. 87, Nov.–Dec., 1984, p. 51.

≪ EDITORIAL SERVICES ≫

Books

R.R. Bowker, *The Literary Marketplace,* New York: R.R. Bowker Company, 1987.

Writer's Digest Books, *Writer's Market: Where to Sell What You Write,* Cincinnati, OH: Writer's Digest Books, 1987.

Magazines

Publishers Weekly, Bowker Magazine Group, Cahners Magazine Division, 205 East 42nd Street, New York, NY 10016.

The Writer, The Writer, Inc., 120 Boylston Street, Boston, MA 02116.

Writer's Digest, F & W Publications, 9933 Alliance Road, Cincinnati, OH 45242.

≪ EXOTICS ≫

Books

Dominitz, Ben & Dominitz, Nancy, *Travel Free! How to Start and Succeed in Your Own Travel Consultant Business,* Rocklin, CA: Prima Publishing/Interbook, 1984.

Elliott, Tom, *Clowns, Clients & Chaos: Starting a Hometown Talent Agency for Fun & Profit,* Boston, MA: TEP, 1983.

Image Industry Publications, *Directory of Personal Image Consultants,* 1986–1987, Staten Island, NY: 1986.

Timberlake, Joan, *Image Consulting: The New Career,* Washington, D.C.: Acropolis Books, 1987.

Trupp, Philip Z., *Tracking Treasure: Romance & Fortune Beneath the Sea and How to Find It!,* Washington, D.C.: Acropolis Books, 1987.

Magazine Articles

American Banker, "Sherlock of the Street: NFS Services Trails Missing Assets from Financial Firms," vol. 149, Oct. 15, 1984, p. 12.

Fund Raising Management, "Should You be Interested in Becoming a Consultant," vol. 17, Feb., 1987, p. 86.

Pet Supplies and Marketing, "The Animal Behavior Consultant," vol. 40, Sept., 1986, p. 48.

Travel Weekly, "Wearing a Meeting Consultant's Hat," vol. 5, Nov. 20, 1986, p. 29.

≪ FINANCIAL PLANNER/INSURANCE ≫

Book

Wyatt, *The Financial Planner's Guide to Publicity & Promotion,* Longman Financial Series, Rockville Centre, NY: Farnsworth Publishing Company, 1986.

Magazine Articles

Business Insurance, "Becoming a Consultant Can Be Risky Business," vol. 20, March 17, 1986, p. 7.

National Underwriter, "An Agent Converts to Consulting," July 4, 1986, p. 3.

———, "'Can Do' Consultants Help Promote Agencies," Oct. 18, 1985, p. 24.

———, "Direct Mail Marketing Predicted to Bring in 20 Percent of Life Insurance Business," Nov. 1, 1986, p. 3.

The New York Times, "The Life of Investor Relations," vol. 136, Nov. 18, 1986, p. D29.

≪ MEDICAL ≫

American Druggist, "Consultant Pharmacy: Risks and Challenges in the First Year," vol. 193, April, 1986, p. 46.

———, "Consultant Services Appeal to Some Drug Chains," vol. 194, October, 1986, p. 148.

Drug Topics, "Long-Term Care Market Enters Era of Specialization," vol. 130, Dec. 15, 1986, p. 106.

Medical Lab Observer, "Needed: Consultants to Physicians Office Labs," parts I & II, vols. 17 & 18, Sept. & Oct., 1985.

≪ PERSONAL FINANCE ≫

This section is designed to help freelance professionals find sources to help them better plan their own financial development.

Brownstone, David M. & Sartisky, Jacques, *The Manager's Lifelong Money Book: A Complete Guide to Personal Financial Planning for Business People,* New York: AMACOM, 1986.

Connell, John R., et al., *Touche Ross Guide to Personal Financial Management,* rev. ed., Englewood Cliffs, N.J.: Prentice-Hall, 1987.

Financial Publishing Co. Staff, *Personal Financial Planner,* Boston: Financial Publishing Co., 1986.

Long, Charles, *How To Survive Without a Salary,* rev. ed., New York: Sterling Books, 1986.

Shane, Dorlene V., *Be Your Own Financial Planner: The 21-Day Guide to Financial Success,* New York: John Wiley & Sons, 1986.

≪ PUBLIC RELATIONS, PROMOTION & PUBLICITY ≫

Books

Carlson, Linda, *The Publicity & Promotion Handbook: A Complete Guide for Small Business,* New York: Van Nostrand Reinhold, 1982.

Knessel, Dave, *Free Publicity: A Step-By-Step Guide,* New York: Sterling Books, 1982.

Parkhurst, William, *How to Get Publicity (And Make the Most of It Once You've Got It),* New York: Times Books, 1985.

Scott, Dewitt H., *Getting Favorable Publicity: The Marketing Tool That Costs You Nothing,* includes six audio cassettes, Los Alamitos, CA: Duncliffs International, 1985.

Stanley, Richard E., *Promotion: Advertising, Publicity, Personal Selling, Sales Promotion,* 2nd ed., Englewood Cliffs, N.J.: Prentice-Hall, 1987.

Weiner, Richard, *The Professional's Guide to Publicity,* 3rd, rev. ed., New York: Public Relations Society of America, 1982.

Weiss, Bonnie, *How To Publicize Your Way To Success,* Gwynedd Valley, PA: Catalyst Publications, 1985.

Magazine Articles

Bank Marketing, "The Three Cs of Effective PR: Control, Consistency and Candor," vol. 14, November, 1984, p. 22.

Communications World, "Entrepreneurs with an Edge," vol. 2, March, 1986, p. 17.

————, "Starting Your Own Business: 4 Success Stories," vol. 3, September, 1986, p. 14.

————, "Suddenly Out on Your Own," vol. 2, August, 1985, p. 33.

INC., "Playing for Position: Regis McKenna on Creating a Marketing Campaign," vol. 7, April, 1985, p. 92.

Public Relations Journal, "CHECKLIST: Getting Your News Releases Through," vol. 42, November, 1986, p. 57.

————, "How to Be Small and Successful," vol. 42, December, 1986, p. 31.

————, "How to Develop a Strategic Plan," vol. 42, April, 1987, p. 31.

————, "How to Get More Mileage from Your Meetings," vol. 42, July, 1986, p. 31.

————, "How to Get the Most Out of a News Conference," vol. 42, September, 1986, p. 33.

————, "How to Get Your Articles Published," vol. 42, February, 1986, p. 35.

————, "How to Make PR Count," vol. 42, May, 1986, p. 31.

≪ RETIREMENT PLANNING ≫

This section helps freelance professionals plan for their retirement.

Action for Older Persons, Inc. Staff, *Your Retirement: How to Plan for a Secure Future,* New York: Arco, 1984.

American Association of Retired Persons, *Retirement Planning Handbook,* Washington, D.C.: AARP, 1984.

AARP Workers Equity Department, *Looking Ahead: How to Plan Your Successful Retirement,* Washington, D.C.: American Association of Retired Persons, 1987.

Bradford, Leland P., *Preparing for Retirement: A Program for Survival—A Participant's Workbook,* San Diego, CA: University Associates, 1981.

Chapman, Elwood N., *Comfort Zones: A Practical Guide for Pre-Retirement Planning,* Los Altos, CA: Crisp Publications, 1985.

Dickinson, Peter A., *The Complete Retirement Planning Book,* New York: Dutton, 1984.

Hack, Stuart, Retirement Planning for Professionals, *Tax & Business Guides for Professionals Series,* New York: John Wiley & Sons, 1986.

J.K. Lasser Tax Institute, *All You Should Know About IRA, Keogh & Other Retirement Plans,* rev. ed., Englewood Cliffs, N.J.: Prentice-Hall, 1987.

Pilot Staff, *Your Personal Guide to Pre-Retirement Planning,* Babylon, NY: Pilot Books, 1983.

Studt R. & Adams, J.M., *Retirement: Planning Tomorrow Today,* New York: McGraw-Hill, 1982.

Vicker, Ray, *The Dow Jones-Irwin Guide to Retirement Planning,* 2nd ed., Homewood, IL.: Dow Jones-Irwin, 1987.

≪ SELF-EMPLOYMENT ≫

Books

Bly, Robert W. and Blake, Gary, *Out on Your Own: From Corporate to Self-Employment,* New York: John Wiley, 1986.

Dorland, Gilbert N. and Ven Der Wal, John, *The Business Idea: From Birth to Profitable Company,* New York: Van Nostrand Reinhold, 1982.

Fregly, Bert, *How to Be Self-Employed,* Palm Springs, CA: ETC Publications, 1977.

Professional Report Editors and Kirk, John, *Incorporating Your Business: The Complete Guide That Tells All You Should Know About Establishing & Operating a Small Corporation,* Chicago: Contemporary Books, 1986.

Rothberg, Diane S. and Cook, Barbara Ensor, *Part-Time Professional,* Washington, D.C.: Acropolis Books, 1987.

Tabares, E.F., *How to Be Employed and Make a Spectacular Success in an Extra Business of Your Own Which You May Conduct in Your Spare Time,* Chicago: Institute of Economics and Finances, 1982.

Magazine Articles

Changing Times, "Start-Up Help for Your Business," vol. 41, June, 1987, p. 73.

Executive Female, "What Are You Waiting For? Don't Let Overplanning Delay Your Business Start-Up," vol. 9, Jan. 2, 1986, p. 45.

INC., "Beyond the Billable Hour: Selling Professional Services," vol. 8, August, 1986, p. 56.

————, "PERSONAL BUSINESS: Founders of Professional Service Firms Have a Choice to Make—Do They Want to Be the Company, or Do They Want to Build One?" vol. 7, April, 1985, p. 68.

Nation's Business, "Taking the Leap," vol. 74, March, 1986, p. 24.

The Professional Report, "Eight Steps to Success When You Work for Yourself," vol. 15, April, 1985, p. 3.

≪ SMALL BUSINESS FINANCE AND MANAGEMENT ≫

Books

Bernstein, Peter W., Ed., *The Arthur Young Tax Guide 1987,* New York: Ballantine Books, 1986.

Carpenter, Donna S., *Laventhol & Horwath Planning Guide for Small Business Owners & Professionals,* New York: Bantam Books, 1986.

Cohen, William A., and Marshall E. Reddick, *Successful Marketing for Small Business,* New York: American Management Association, 1981.

Coltman, Michael M., *Financial Control for the Small Business: A Practical Primer for Keeping a Tighter Rein on Your Profits and Cash Flow,* Blue Ridge Summit, PA: TAB Books, 1982.

Ellis, John, *The New Financial Guide for the Self-Employed,* Chicago: Contemporary Books, 1981.

Grollman, William K., *The Accountant as Business Advisor,* New York: John Wiley & Sons, 1986.

Hayes, Stephen R. & Howell, John C., *How to Finance Your Small Business with Government Money: SBA & Other Loans,* 2nd ed., Small Business Management Series, New York: John Wiley & Sons, 1983.

Ireland, LaVerne H., *The Small Business Expense Planner,* Davis, CA: Petervin Press, 1984.

Laventhol & Horwath, *Laventhol & Horwath's Small Business Tax Preparation Guide,* New York: Bantam Books, 1987.

Lowery, Albert J., *How to Become Financially Successful by Owning Your Own Business*, New York: Simon and Schuster, 1981.

Nierenberg, Gerald I., *Fundamentals of Negotiating*, New York: Hawthorn Books, 1973.

_____, *How to Give & Receive Advice*, New York: Pocket Books, 1975.

Pope, Jeffrey, *Practical Marketing Research*, New York: American Management Association, 1981.

Pratt, Stanley E., *How To Raise Venture Capital*, New York: Charles Scribner's Sons, 1982.

Professional Report Editors & Kirk, John, *Incorporating Your Business: The Complete Guide that Tells All You Should Know About Establishing & Operating A Small Corporation*, Chicago: Contemporary Books, 1986.

Ragan, Robert C. and Zwick, Jack, *Fundamentals of Recordkeeping & Finance for the Small Business*, Englewood Cliffs, N.J.: Reston, 1978.

Rausch, Edward N., *Financial Keys to Small Business Profitability*, New York: American Management Association, 1982.

Schaefer, Robert A., *Starting & Managing a Small Service Business*, *Vol. 101, Starting & Managing Series*, Washington, D.C.: U.S. Government Printing Office, 1986.

Shenson, Howard L., *How to Strategically Negotiate the Consulting Contract*, Washington, D.C.: Bermont Books, 1980.

Silver, A. David, *Up-Front Financing: Entrepreneur's Guide*, Wiley Series on Small Business Management, New York: John Wiley & Sons, 1985.

Toncre, Emery, *Maximizing Cash Flow: Practical Financial Control for Your Business*, Small Business Management Series, New York: The Ronald Press, dist. John Wiley & Sons, 1986.

U.S. Government Printing Office, *Financial Management: How to Make a Go of Your Business*, Small Business Management Series, Series 44, Washington, D.C.: US GPO, 1986.

Magazine Articles

Business Owner, "A Banker Explains the Right Way to Get a Loan, Why Some Are Rejected," vol. 9, April, 1985, p. 10.

_____, "New Money: How to Determine If It Pays to Borrow," vol. 10, October, 1986, p. 15.

INC., "The One-Minute Lender," vol. 6, December, 1984, p. 150.

Journal of Accounting, "Finding Funds for a Small Business," vol. 162, August, 1986, p. 114.

Management Accounting, "Financing Your Business," vol. 68, February, 1987, p. 50.

New England Business, "Angels Give Wing to Entrepreneurs," vol. 8, Dec. 1, 1986, p. 31.

The Professional Report, "How to Make the Right Moves When You Want to Borrow from the Bank," vol. 16, February, 1986, p. 11.

————, "More Women Own Businesses But Problems Remain," vol. 16, July, 1986, p. 12.

Profit & Business Strategies for Business Owners, "A Commercial Line of Credit: Assurance You Can Get Cash When You Need It," vol. 16, December, 1986, p. 12.

Savvy, "Anchor a Banker," vol. 7, November, 1986, p. 66.

Wall Street Journal, "More States Establish Venture Networks," April 13, 1987, p. 25.

Working Woman, "Business Plans: What Turns Investors On, What Turns Them Off: Eight Key Dos and Don'ts to Make Your Business Plan a Winner," vol. 11, January, 1986, p. 38.

————, "How Healthy Is Your Business? These 8 Ratios Help You Figure That Out," vol. 12, January, 1987, p. 39.

≪ CREDIT AND COLLECTIONS ≫

The Professional Report, "Mistakes That May Make It Harder to Collect What Customers Owe You," vol. 15, March, 1985, p. 9.

≪ TECHNICAL AND SCIENTIFIC CONSULTING ≫

Black Enterprise, "High-Tech Consulting," vol. 17, April, 1987, p. 27.

New York Times, "Technical Consultants Snarled by Tax Law," vol. 136, Jan. 28, 1987, p. 34.

Technical Communications, Special issue on freelancing, vol. 33, November, 1986, pages 206–248. Includes these articles: "Beginner's Guide to Freelancing," p. 209; "Consultant, Freelancer, Contractor: Take Your Choice," p. 218; "The Technical Writer as a Consultant," p. 215.

Washington Post, "IRS Issues Guidelines for Consultants," vol. 110, Jan. 22, 1987, p. C5.

Electronic Design News (EDN), "A New Tax Law Polarizes the Technical-Consulting Community," vol. 32, June 11, 1987, p. 269.

≪ TELEMARKETING AND TELEPHONE SELLING ≫

This section gives books and articles that may help freelance professionals perfect their telephone selling and telemarketing skills.

Books

Goodman, Gary, *Reach Out and Sell Someone: Phone Your Way to Success Through the Goodman System of Telemarketing,* Englewood Cliffs, N.J.: Prentice-Hall, 1983.

Pope, Jeffrey L., *Business-to-Business Telephone Marketing,* New York: AMACOM, 1983.

Porterfield, James D., *Sell on the Phone: A Self-Teaching Guide, Teaching Guides Series,* New York: Wiley Press, 1985.

Telemarketing Magazine Staff, *Telemarketing's One Hundred Do's and Don'ts,* New York: Technical Marketing, 1986.

Watras, Jan, *Building Sales Through Telemarketing,* Hinsdale, IL: Continuing Education Systems, 1987.

Magazine Articles

Direct Marketing, "Getting the Most Out of Telemarketing," vol. 50, June, 1987, p. 34.

————, "Inside or Outside? Launching a Telemarketing Operation," vol. 49, March, 1987, p. 100.

Public Relations Journal, "How to Use Telemarketing," vol. 41, October, 1985, p. 31.

≪ TRAINING ≫

Training and Development Journal, "What Do Consultant Trainers Need to Know to Be Successful? (Guidelines for Successful Consultants), vol. 41, April, 1987, p. 26.

INDEX